OPPOSING
VIEWPOINTS®
SERIES

Mass Media

Other Books of Related Interest

Opposing Viewpoints Series

Internet Censorship

Journalism

Netiquette and Online Ethics

Smartphones

At Issue Series

Location-Based Social Networking and Services

Negative Campaigning

Reality TV

What Is the Impact of Twitter?

Current Controversies Series

E-books

Internet Activism

Politics and Religion

Violence in the Media

"Congress shall make
no law . . . abridging
the freedom of speech,
or of the press."

First Amendment to the US Constitution

The basic foundation of our democracy is the First Amendment guarantee of freedom of expression. The Opposing Viewpoints Series is dedicated to the concept of this basic freedom and the idea that it is more important to practice it than to enshrine it.

OPPOSING
VIEWPOINTS®
SERIES

Mass Media

Margaret Haerens and Lynn M. Zott, Book Editors

GREENHAVEN PRESS
A part of Gale, Cengage Learning

GALE
CENGAGE Learning·

Farmington Hills, Mich • San Francisco • New York • Waterville, Maine
Meriden, Conn • Mason, Ohio • Chicago

GALE
CENGAGE Learning·

Elizabeth Des Chenes, *Director, Content Strategy*
Cynthia Sanner, *Publisher*
Douglas Dentino, *Manager, New Product*

© 2014 Greenhaven Press, a part of Gale, Cengage Learning.

WCN: 01-100-101

Articles in Greenhaven Press anthologies are often edited for length to meet page requirements. In addition, original titles of these works are changed to clearly present the main thesis and to explicitly indicate the author's opinion. Every effort is made to ensure that Greenhaven Press accurately reflects the original intent of the authors. Every effort has been made to trace the owners of copyrighted material.

Cover image © VLADGRIN/Shutterstock.com.

LIBRARY OF CONGRESS CATALOGING-IN-PUBLICATION DATA

Mass media / Margaret Haerens and Lynn M. Zott, book editors.
     p. cm. -- (Opposing viewpoints)
     Includes bibliographical references and index.
     Includes webliography.
     ISBN 978-0-7377-6660-8 (hardcover) -- ISBN 978-0-7377-6661-5 (pbk.)
     1. Mass media. I. Haerens, Margaret editor of compilation. II. Zott, Lynn M.
(Lynn Marie), 1969- editor of compilation.
     P87.25.M37 2014
     302.23--dc23
                                                              2013032063

Printed in the United States of America
1 2 3 4 5   18 17 16 15 14

Contents

4/14 30.95
Cengage Learning

Chapter 3: How Do the Media Affect Society?

Chapter 4: What Is the Future of Mass Media?

Why Consider Opposing Viewpoints?

> *"The only way in which a human being can make some approach to knowing the whole of a subject is by hearing what can be said about it by persons of every variety of opinion and studying all modes in which it can be looked at by every character of mind. No wise man ever acquired his wisdom in any mode but this."*
>
> *John Stuart Mill*

In our media-intensive culture it is not difficult to find differing opinions. Thousands of newspapers and magazines and dozens of radio and television talk shows resound with differing points of view. The difficulty lies in deciding which opinion to agree with and which "experts" seem the most credible. The more inundated we become with differing opinions and claims, the more essential it is to hone critical reading and thinking skills to evaluate these ideas. Opposing Viewpoints books address this problem directly by presenting stimulating debates that can be used to enhance and teach these skills. The varied opinions contained in each book examine many different aspects of a single issue. While examining these conveniently edited opposing views, readers can develop critical thinking skills such as the ability to compare and contrast authors' credibility, facts, argumentation styles, use of persuasive techniques, and other stylistic tools. In short, the Opposing Viewpoints Series is an ideal way to attain the higher-level thinking and reading skills so essential in a culture of diverse and contradictory opinions.

In addition to providing a tool for critical thinking, Opposing Viewpoints books challenge readers to question their own strongly held opinions and assumptions. Most people form their opinions on the basis of upbringing, peer pressure, and personal, cultural, or professional bias. By reading carefully balanced opposing views, readers must directly confront new ideas as well as the opinions of those with whom they disagree. This is not to simplistically argue that everyone who reads opposing views will—or should—change his or her opinion. Instead, the series enhances readers' understanding of their own views by encouraging confrontation with opposing ideas. Careful examination of others' views can lead to the readers' understanding of the logical inconsistencies in their own opinions, perspective on why they hold an opinion, and the consideration of the possibility that their opinion requires further evaluation.

Evaluating Other Opinions

To ensure that this type of examination occurs, Opposing Viewpoints books present all types of opinions. Prominent spokespeople on different sides of each issue as well as well-known professionals from many disciplines challenge the reader. An additional goal of the series is to provide a forum for other, less known, or even unpopular viewpoints. The opinion of an ordinary person who has had to make the decision to cut off life support from a terminally ill relative, for example, may be just as valuable and provide just as much insight as a medical ethicist's professional opinion. The editors have two additional purposes in including these less known views. One, the editors encourage readers to respect others' opinions—even when not enhanced by professional credibility. It is only by reading or listening to and objectively evaluating others' ideas that one can determine whether they are worthy of consideration. Two, the inclusion of such viewpoints encourages the important critical thinking skill of objectively evaluating an author's credentials and bias. This evaluation will illuminate an author's reasons for taking a particular stance on an issue and will aid in readers' evaluation of the author's ideas.

It is our hope that these books will give readers a deeper understanding of the issues debated and an appreciation of the complexity of even seemingly simple issues when good and honest people disagree. This awareness is particularly important in a democratic society such as ours in which people enter into public debate to determine the common good. Those with whom one disagrees should not be regarded as enemies but rather as people whose views deserve careful examination and may shed light on one's own.

Thomas Jefferson once said that "difference of opinion leads to inquiry, and inquiry to truth." Jefferson, a broadly educated man, argued that "if a nation expects to be ignorant and free . . . it expects what never was and never will be." As individuals and as a nation, it is imperative that we consider the opinions of others and examine them with skill and discernment. The Opposing Viewpoints Series is intended to help readers achieve this goal.

David L. Bender and Bruno Leone,
Founders

Introduction

"The public lives in a world where it seems impossible to know what is fact and what is partisan fiction."

—Julian Zelizer,
"Do Facts Matter?," CNN.com,
October 16, 2012

One of the biggest trends in news media since about 2007 has been the rise of fact-checking. By 2012, fact-checking was everywhere: there were dozens of point-by-point analyses of speeches made at the Republican and Democratic National Conventions, comments uttered at presidential debates, and political ads aired on TV. Fact-checking became a feature of most major national newspapers and the major cable TV news stations. Fact-checking was so ubiquitous during the run up to the 2012 presidential election that it finally generated a strong backlash from the political community. Political operatives and media pundits began to question the rise of fact-checking and the motives behind it. Some political campaigns, including that of the Republican candidate for president, Mitt Romney, made a strategic decision to ignore the conclusions of fact-checkers. During the Republican National Convention, Romney pollster Neil Newhouse suggested that fact-checking groups had a liberal media bias and could not be trusted to give a fair analysis of Romney's political message. "Fact-checkers come to this with their own sets of thoughts and beliefs, and we're not going to let our campaign be dictated by fact-checkers," Newhouse fumed.

The rise of fact-checking is generally credited to a growing suspicion of the American news media. Polls show that an increasing percentage of Americans are not satisfied with the quality of news coverage available. In a Gallup poll published in September 2012, distrust of the mainstream media was revealed to be at an all-time high. Gallup reported that 60 percent of Americans polled stated that they have little or no trust in the mass media to report the news fully, accurately, and fairly.

Most of that negative perception was reported by Republicans, who had the least amount of trust in the media in general. Many of them suggested that the news media had a liberal bias, and that reporters generally favored Democratic candidates over Republicans. During the 2012 presidential election, conservatives argued that Barack Obama got an overwhelming advantage from flattering media coverage, while Mitt Romney was pounded by unfair negative reporting. On radio, television, and in print, conservative commentators constantly pointed to liberal media bias and seethed about its effect on electoral politics and cultural and social issues.

Other commentators suggested that in an attempt to provide unbiased and balanced news coverage, the media was not doing a good job in identifying inaccuracies and distortions. The media had become so sensitive to charges of liberal media bias that they were failing to criticize conservative politicians or media figures for outrageous lies and misleading statements. "For years, Americans' political press has been stuck in a fact-free model of neutrality, often covering even the most obvious lies as 'one side' of a dispute," observes MSNBC analyst Ari Melber. "From Swift Boats to global warming to Iraq's nonexistent WMDs [weapons of mass destruction], this coverage shrouds even rudimentary empirical claims in a fog of truthiness."

As trust in the news media plummeted, news organizations and media institutions began to explore ways to win back the public's confidence. One of the most obvious strategies was the establishment of impartial and first-rate fact-checking services as a prominent part of news coverage. By analyzing the claims of both conservative and liberal politicians, these supposedly independent fact-checkers aimed to dispel the growing reputation of the media as unfair and biased.

Of course, fact-checking has always had a place in modern news media. Throughout the years, many organizations have performed some level of fact-checking as a feature of their news coverage. But what was being proposed now were independent arms of news organizations or media institutions that would be devoted to the act of analyzing political ads, speeches, testimony, debates, and other statements found to be newsworthy or relevant to the general interest. The first major fact-checking project, FactCheck.org, was established in 2003 by the Annenberg Public Policy Center of the University of Pennsylvania. Calling itself a "consumer advocate" working on behalf of American voters, Factcheck.org stated that it determined to "reduce the level of deception and confusion in US politics. We monitor the factual accuracy of what is said by major US political players in the form of TV ads, debates, speeches, interviews, and news releases. Our goal is to apply the best practices of both journalism and scholarship, and to increase public knowledge and understanding."

In August 2007 another major fact-checking project, PolitiFact.com, was started by the *Tampa Bay Times* in conjunction with the *Congressional Quarterly*. Reporters and editors rate political claims for their accuracy and evaluate the progress made to fulfill promises made by politicians. For example, PolitiFact.com features an "Obamameter," which tracks President Obama's performance related to his campaign promises. PolitiFact.com received the Pulitzer Prize for National Reporting in 2009 for its "fact-checking initiative during the 2008 presidential campaign that used probing reporters and the power of the World Wide Web to examine more than 750 political claims, separating rhetoric from truth to enlighten voters."

In September 2007, *The Washington Post* launched its own fact-checking project, The Fact Checker, to provide coverage of the 2008 presidential campaign. CNN also began to feature fact-checking segments and a CNN Fact Check on its website, providing in-depth analysis of political statements. Other news media organizations followed. By the 2012 presidential election, fact-checking had become a regular feature of news coverage, influencing political campaigns and media strategies. As *New York Times* reporter David Carr observed, "As so many media outlets promised, this was indeed the most fact-checked election in history. At any given moment within the last 18 months, there were so many truth squadrons in the air that mid-air collisions seemed a genuine possibility."

The authors of the viewpoints included in *Opposing Viewpoints: Mass Media* debate the role and future of media under the following chapter headings: What Should Be the Role of the News Media?, Are the News Media Biased?, How Do the Media Affect Society?, and What Is the Future of Mass Media? The volume explores the influence of the media on American politics and culture and takes a look at the technology that is expected to determine the future of mass media.

CHAPTER 1

What Should Be the Role of the News Media?

Chapter Preface

In the final stretch of the 2012 US presidential campaign, controversy erupted over the airing of a political ad on television titled "Right Choice." Created by the Mitt Romney campaign, the television ad attacked President Barack Obama's 2012 decision to exempt some states from welfare requirements. The ad charged: "In 1996, President Clinton and a bipartisan Congress helped end welfare as we know it by requiring work for welfare. But on July 12, President Obama quietly announced a plan to gut welfare reform by dropping work requirements. Under Obama's plan, you wouldn't have to work and wouldn't have to train for a job. They just send you your welfare check. And welfare-to-work goes back to being plain old welfare. Mitt Romney will restore the work requirement because it works."

Polls showed that many Republicans and independent voters viewed "Right Choice" as one of the campaign's most effective ads. It raised concerns that President Obama was erasing the welfare reforms of 1996 and returning to welfare programs that fostered fraud and waste. It played into stereotypes of Democratic candidates as being more concerned with providing costly entitlements and encouraging dependency on Big Government than being financially conservative and getting people off welfare. Most importantly, defenders perceived the ad as accurate: President Obama had waived the work requirements for welfare in some states—and many believed that he did not have the authority to change the rules under the existing law.

However, the popularity and effectiveness of "Right Choice" was quickly overshadowed by concerns over its accuracy. Fact-checking organizations analyzed the ad and pointed out that some of the claims were not completely true. The Obama administration was proposing to exempt specific states from welfare requirements if they were able to present a well-crafted and measurable plan to get welfare recipients back to work. Some states had requested such waivers from the federal government, arguing that the states had more of an incentive to get people off of welfare and could do a better job in formulating effective work or training programs. The federal waiver would give state lawmakers the flexibility to formulate programs that would better fit their needs as long as they met or exceeded certain performance standards. In the analysis of the major fact-checkers, it was simply not true that President Obama had "gutted welfare reform."

Despite failing ratings from fact-checking organizations, the Romney campaign continued to air "Right Choice" in several media markets. They did it because it worked: it significantly appealed to independent voters, a much-needed voting bloc for Mitt Romney. "Our most effective ad is our welfare ad," Republican strategist Ashley O'Connor stated at a Republican National Committee forum in late August 2012. "It's new information."

Republicans went on the attack against fact-checking organizations, dismissing the controversy over the accuracy of "Right Choice" as the work of political partisans and biased media. During an event at the Republican National Convention, Romney pollster Neil Newhouse suggested that factchecking groups had a liberal media bias and could not be trusted to give a fair analysis of Romney's political message. "Fact checkers come to this with their own sets of thoughts and beliefs, and we're not going to let our campaign be dictated by fact checkers," Newhouse stated.

The debate over fact-checking and the role of news media is the subject of the following chapter. Other viewpoints examine the news media's success in informing the American public of major global news and its attitude toward traditional moral values.

| *"Journalists rightly espouse a creed that their highest duty is to the truth."*

Ignored Factchecks and the Media's Crisis of Conscience

Brendan Nyhan

Brendan Nyhan is an assistant professor of government at Dartmouth College, a blogger, and a political columnist. In the following viewpoint, he acknowledges a crisis of confidence in journalistic fact-checking circles after political campaigns continued to put out misleading and inaccurate ads during the 2012 election cycle. Nyhan asserts that fact-checking is an essential role of journalists, who must be more effective in calling out patterns of lies and misleading statements. He argues that journalism has a responsibility to the truth, even if readers accuse them of bias or grandstanding in the process.

As you read, consider the following questions:

1. How many times does Nyhan estimate that Mitt Romney's misleading welfare ad had run by August 23, 2012?

2. What two *New York Times* reporters does the author identify as effectively reminding readers that the welfare ad was bogus?

3. According to Nyhan, what *Daily Beast* reporter focused more on the effectiveness of Paul Ryan's convention speech than its accuracy?

Can the media stop politicians from misleading the public?

That's the question on the minds of many journalists and commentators after Paul Ryan's speech last night [August 29, 2012,] at the Republican [GOP] National Convention, which continued the Romney campaign's pattern of disingenuous and misleading attacks on President Obama. While Obama and his allies have made many misleading claims of their own, the frequency and repetition of the Romney campaign's claims has been particularly striking.

The debate over the GOP ticket's lack of responsiveness to factchecking first attracted widespread attention earlier this week after a pollster for Romney waved away criticism of a television ad falsely accusing President Obama of undermining work requirements for welfare. As Ben Smith reported in *BuzzFeed*:

> *The Washington Post*'s "Fact Checker" awarded Romney's ad "four Pinocchios," a measure Romney pollster Neil Newhouse dismissed.

> "Fact checkers come to this with their own sets of thoughts and beliefs, and we're not going to let our campaign be dictated by fact checkers," he said. The fact-checkers—whose institutional rise has been a feature of the cycle—have "jumped the shark," he added after the panel.

The Romney crew has heavily featured the welfare ad, which strategist Ashley O'Connor called the campaign's "most effective," despite criticism from all three major fact-checkers.

(Interestingly, Romney has previously cited these institutions' work when it serves his purposes.) As of August 23, the welfare ad had run nearly 6,000 times. The chutzpah [brazenness] Ryan showed last night suggests that Romney's campaign remains unbowed by the criticism it has faced.

This brazen disregard of pushback from journalists has brought on the latest episode in a recurring crisis of confidence among media types. Politicians have persisted in misleading claims before, but the ubiquity of online debunking in this cycle has brought the disjunction into sharper relief, as this chronology by NYU [New York University] professor and media critic Jay Rosen highlights:

> If we start back in the 1990s and read forward to the current campaign, we see distinct phases of innovation as political journalists react to misleading ads: first, the ad watch phase in the 90s; there was some mention of misleading elements, but the final tally was about effectiveness, or what I call "savvy." The limitations of the ad watch led to direct fact-checking by the press, where actual grades are handed out. The emphasis is on judging truth and falsehood, not assessing effectiveness. So now we're in a new phase: fact checking alone is not enough. The campaigns seem able to override it . . .

The Washington Post's Dan Balz was similarly pessimistic two weeks ago:

> News organizations instituted fact-checking and ad watches in reaction to earlier campaigns, when candidates were getting away with half-truths and worse, with little accountability. These have become robust and increasingly comprehensive. But they are not providing much of a check on the campaigns' behavior.

This attention to the effectiveness of journalistic strategies is appropriate. In my view, though, we should rejoice that the inaccuracy of Romney's ad is a continued topic of debate, not

The Fact-Checking Trend

The fact-checking explosion may have begun in 2004 after the media's initially flat-footed response to the attacks on [Democratic presidential candidate] Sen. John Kerry by the group that called itself Swift Boat Veterans for Truth. But the just-completed 2010 election featured fact-checking on steroids. A bitterly divided electorate and a political landscape replete with high-decibel claims and counterclaims on cable television and echoing throughout the blogosphere have made neutral arbiters more crucial than ever.

"I never thought journalism would be like this," says Bill Adair, the *St. Petersburg Times'* Washington, D.C., bureau chief and editor of PolitiFact, the Pulitzer Prize-winning fact-checking operation that is exporting its approach to local news operations across the country. "It's just the right formula for the new era."

Cary Spivak, American Journalism Review,
December–January 2011.

fall into despair or paralysis over the media's failure to dictate the content of a presidential campaign. The underlying problem with these analyses is the misguided conclusion that factchecking is a failure if it does not *eliminate* deception. From a scientific perspective, however, factchecking is effective if it reduces the prevalence of misleading claims relative to an otherwise identical world that lacks factchecking, which seems likely to be the case (though we lack direct evidence on this point).

With that said, journalists could be *more* effective in responding to a pattern of false claims. First, they should remember to continue to remind readers—some of whom are just starting to tune into the campaign—that claims like those in the welfare ad are bogus. Jeff Zeleny and Jim Rutenberg did exactly that in a *New York Times* report last weekend that flatly described the ad as "falsely charging that Mr. Obama has 'quietly announced' plans to eliminate work and job training requirements for welfare beneficiaries." Likewise, in a blog item that was later published in print, the *Times*'s Michael Cooper reminded readers that the Republican convention featured a "selectively edited" clip of President Obama's "you didn't build that" statement, which was made all the way back in July.

Second, as *The Atlantic*'s Garance Franke-Ruta has argued, reporters should cover a pattern of false claims as an ongoing story rather than ignoring it as old news. For instance, a widely lauded *Los Angeles Times* [LAT] story highlighted by Rosen focused on former Pennsylvania senator Rick Santorum's repetition of the false welfare claim in his speech at the convention Tuesday. Under the headline "Rick Santorum repeats inaccurate welfare attack on Obama," the *LAT*'s David Lauter notes in his third paragraph that Santorum's "reprise of an inaccurate Romney campaign attack on Obama over welfare" gave his speech "its hardest edge." This is the sort of story that, over time, can threaten a politician's reputation for truth-telling.

But while journalists have recently produced some strong work about truth and lies in the campaign, the morning-after coverage of Ryan's speech in the mainstream media is largely an example of what *not* to do. Leading outlets largely buried or ignored the vice presidential nominee's hypocritical and misleading criticism of Medicare spending cuts (which his own budget assumes) and his attack on Obama for not embracing the recommendations of the Simpson-Bowles deficit commission (which Ryan himself opposed). Instead, the reporting tended to focus, as *The Daily Beast*'s Howard Kurtz did, on theater critic–style analysis of the effectiveness of the speech. (Kurtz slipped a brief discussion of Ryan's "cynically selective attack" on Obama into the eighth paragraph of his analysis.)

Of course, there is no magic bullet here. Given current levels of polarization and media distrust, many voters will remain unpersuaded by factchecks, which in turn reduces the incentive for politicians to care what the media says. But journalists rightly espouse a creed that their highest duty is to the truth, not the marketplace or the people they cover. When someone who could be the next president or vice president of the United States makes a false claim, it is *always* a newsworthy act. Reporters should honor that duty in their coverage.

> *"Anyone who really believes in the authority of 'fact checkers' has a liar's paradox problem."*

News Media Fact-Checking Can Be Selective and Biased

James Taranto

James Taranto is a political columnist and editor at the Wall Street Journal. *In the following viewpoint, he contends that media fact-checking can be heavily biased and poorly done. Taranto points to several examples from the 2012 presidential campaign, arguing that fact-checkers often exhibited their biases by judging the quality of the argument and not the veracity of the claims. Therefore, Taranto says, these fact-checking operations effectively took sides in a partisan political dispute. He views this as another sign of the inexorable decline of mainstream journalism, an institution that he believes has managed to blur the line between fact and propaganda.*

As you read, consider the following questions:

1. What two fact-checking operations does Taranto identify as rigorous and the best known?

2. What fact-checker does Taranto deem "the worst of a bad lot"?

3. According to French newspaper *Le Nouvel Observateur,* as cited by the author, who is "the pope of American political journalists"?

In the 19th-century fairy tale "The Adventures of Pinocchio," the eponymous protagonist is a wooden puppet who dreams of becoming an actual boy. We suppose people who work as fact checkers have long dreamed of becoming writers and editors, who enjoy, respectively, the glory and the power in journalism.

Fact Checkers

Outside the world of journalism, fact checkers were pretty much unknown until recently. Like proofreaders, they work behind the scenes. Their job is quality control. The most rigorous fact-checking operations—*The New Yorker*'s and *Reader's Digest*'s are the best known among us who know about such things—would scrutinize every factual assertion in an article, reporting back so that any error could be corrected.

Over the past few years, many organizations have promoted "fact checkers" by making them writers, or perhaps demoted writers by making them fact checkers. No, it's more the former, because other writers have been bowing to the "fact checkers" as submissively as Barack Obama upon meeting some anti-American dictator.

"Fact-checker findings, including those by *The Washington Post*'s project, figure prominently in campaign ads," enthuses a *Post* news story. "The unique rating systems used by these organizations—including the trademarked Truth-O-Meter and Pinocchios—have become part of the political vernacular." A *New York Times* news story laments that fact checkers' "verdicts . . . are often drowned out by dissent."

Voters Divided on Press Influence

In November 2012, the Pew Research Center for People and the Press asked US voters: "How much influence do you think news organizations had on the outcome of this year's presidential election, too much, too little or about the right amount?"

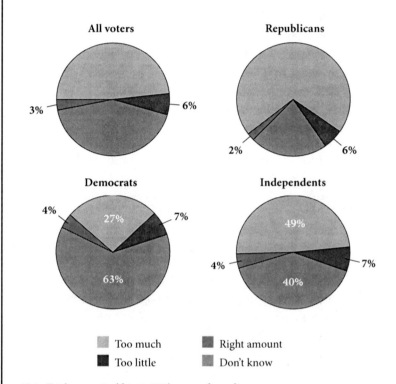

All voters

Republicans

3%   6%

2%   6%

Democrats

Independents

4%   27%   7%

49%

4%   7%

63%   40%

◻ Too much   ◼ Right amount
◼ Too little   ▨ Don't know

Note: Totals may not add up to 100 because of rounding.

TAKEN FROM: Pew Research Center for the People and the Press, "Low Marks for the 2012 Election," November 15, 2012. www.people-press.org.

Perhaps the reason other journalists are so deferential toward the "fact checkers" is that these fact checkers, unlike the traditional ones, don't check the facts of journalists but of politicians. By and large, they aren't actually checking facts but making and asserting judgments about the veracity of politicians' arguments.

The Quality of Fact Checking

The quality of their work is generally quite poor. "The MSM's [mainstream media's] fact-checkers often don't know what they're talking about," notes Mickey Kaus, who cites an example on a subject he knows well:

> The oft-cited CNN "fact check" of Romney's welfare ad makes a big deal of HHS [Health and Human Services] secretary [Kathleen] Sebelius' pledge that she will only grant waivers to states that "commit that their proposals will move at least 20% more people from welfare to work." CNN swallows this 20% Rule whole in the course of declaring Romney's objection "wrong":
>
> "The waivers gave 'those states some flexibility in how they manage their welfare rolls as long as it produced 20% increases in the number of people getting work.'"
>
> Why, it looks as if Obama wants to make the work provisions tougher! Fact-check.org cites the same 20% rule.
>
> I was initially skeptical of Sebelius' 20% pledge, since a) it measures the 20% against "the state's past performance," not what the state's performance would be if it actually tried to comply with the welfare law's requirements as written, and b) Sebelius pulled it out of thin air only after it became clear that the new waiver rule could be a political problem for the president. She could just as easily drop it in the future; and c) Sebelius made it clear the states don't have to actually achieve the 20% goal—only "demonstrate clear progress toward" it.
>
> But Robert Rector, a welfare reform zealot who nevertheless does know what he's talking about, has now published a longer analysis of the 20% rule. Turns out it's not as big a scam as I'd thought it was. It's a much bigger scam.

The merits of the argument are beyond the scope of today's column. It is quite possible that there are people whose knowledge of the subject is as deep as Kaus's and Rector's but whose honest interpretation is more favorable to the Sebelius position. An appeal to their authority could carry as much weight as our appeal to Kaus's and Rector's.

Examples of Recent Fact Checking

But an appeal to the authority of "independent fact checkers" carries no weight at all. In case you're skeptical of this assertion, let's look at some other examples of their output from the past week [late August–early September 2012].

Here's an excerpt from an Associated Press [AP] "fact check" of Paul Ryan's convention speech:

> RYAN: "And the biggest, coldest power play of all in Obamacare came at the expense of the elderly. . . . So they just took it all away from Medicare. Seven hundred and sixteen billion dollars, funneled out of Medicare by President Obama."

> THE FACTS: Ryan's claim ignores the fact that Ryan himself incorporated the same cuts into budgets he steered through the House in the past two years as chairman of its Budget Committee. . . .

> RYAN: "The stimulus was a case of political patronage, corporate welfare and cronyism at their worst. You, the working men and women of this country, were cut out of the deal."

> THE FACTS: Ryan himself asked for stimulus funds shortly after Congress approved the $800 billion plan.

In both of these cases, the AP neither disputes nor verifies the factual accuracy of Ryan's statements. Each of these is simply a *tu quoque*—an argument *against Ryan*. Under the guise of fact checking, the AP is simply taking sides in a partisan political dispute.

The Authority of Fact Checkers

The most disputed portion of Ryan's speech involved the closing of a General Motors plant in his hometown of Janesville,

Wis. An editorial in *The Wall Street Journal* Friday defended Ryan's account against "the press corps' fact checkers" and the liberals who loves them.

But even the so-called fact checkers can't agree on the facts. PolitiFact rated Ryan's account "false," while CNN.com called it "true but incomplete." Anyone who really believes in the authority of "fact checkers" has a liar's paradox problem.[1]

Sometimes the so-called checks are just red herrings. Here's an example from ABC News:

> In comparing President Obama to Jimmy Carter, Ryan said [that] in July 1980 the unemployment rate was 7.8 percent and "for the past 42 months it's been above 8 percent under Barack Obama's failed leadership."

> Both parts of this sentence are true according to the Department of Labor Bureau of Labor Statistics, but in July 1983, when Ronald Reagan was president, unemployment was at 9.4 percent. In July 1982 it was higher at 9.8 percent.

> In July 1992, when George H.W. Bush was president, unemployment was at 7.7 percent.

> Is what Ryan said factually correct? Yes, but it leaves out some important data.

Ryan compared Obama to Carter. ABC thinks he should also (or instead) have compared Obama to Reagan and Bush. There is no factual dispute here whatever.

Sometimes the "fact checkers" are ignorant even of facts that, in contrast with the welfare material above, require no special expertise to know. This is from a CNN.com "fact check":

---

1. The liar's paradox is a problem in logic regarding the truth of the following assertion: "This statement is false." If the statement is deemed to be true, then it is a false statement; if deemed false, then it is a true statement.

In a new policy paper, his Republican rival for the White House, Mitt Romney, says, "President Obama has intentionally sought to shut down oil, gas, and coal production in pursuit of his own alternative energy agenda." . . .

Obama has, for sure, angered some oil and coal producers by steering federal money to alternative energy sources. But there is no evidence that he is trying to "shut down" traditional energy industries.

No evidence? How about Obama's own words? "So, if somebody wants to build a coal-powered plant, they can. It's just that it will bankrupt them, because they're going to be charged a huge sum for all that greenhouse gas that's being emitted."

Sometimes the "fact checkers" simply pronounce trivial truths. From the AP on Mitt Romney's convention speech:

ROMNEY: "I have a plan to create 12 million new jobs. It has five steps."

THE FACTS: No one says he can't, but economic forecasters are divided on his ability to deliver. He'd have to nearly double the anemic pace of job growth lately.

This is like "fact checking" somebody's wedding vows by asserting that while marriage can be wonderful, it's hard work and ends in divorce half the time.

The Worst Case

Among "fact checkers," the worst of a bad lot may be the *Washington Post*'s Glenn Kessler. On Thursday afternoon he actually wrote a post called "Previewing the 'Facts' in Mitt Romney's Acceptance Speech." With those scare quotes, he declared the Republican nominee a liar before Romney had even opened his mouth.

Conservative blogger Stacy McCain describes "the pattern for Republican National Convention coverage: Democrats choose their themes, issue their talking points and their media henchpersons then repeat the partisan spin as if it were a matter of indisputable fact." Kessler didn't wait; he wrote the talking points himself.

The usual conservative complaint about all this "fact-checking" is the same as the conservative complaint about the MSM's product in general: that it is overwhelmingly biased toward the left. But the form amplifies the bias. It gives journalists much freer rein to express their opinions by allowing them to pretend to be rendering authoritative judgments about the facts. The result, as we've seen, is shoddy arguments and shoddier journalism.

Excuses on the Left

The partisan fault-finding directed against Republicans is accompanied by partisan excuse-making for Democrats. Thus ABCNews.com tries yet again to rationalize away Obama's most notorious presidential utterance:

> Greeting Air Force One as it touched down [in Iowa] under sunny skies and sultry heat was a hand-painted banner draped across the top of an airplane hangar that reads, "Obama Welcome to SUX—We Did Build This." "SUX" is the airport code for Sioux City.

> The message appeared to be a response President Obama's "you didn't build that" remark from a July campaign rally, when he was trying to explain that government—not businesses—constructed public infrastructure on which the economy relies.

"Obama is casting his net for the moron vote," wrote R. Emmett Tyrrell in a recent column. "I do not believe that there are enough morons out there to reelect him." But if ABC is right that Obama found it necessary to "explain" that government builds "public infrastructure," the president is also making a play for the idiot vote.

Bad journalism feeds into ever-more-extreme rhetoric from the left. "Last night, Paul Ryan lied to the American people," wrote Brenda Witt of MoveOn.org in a Thursday email. "Some journalists and outlets covered Ryan's lies. But others failed to check the facts and didn't call Ryan out on his brazen lies." *The San Francisco Chronicle* reports:

> Greetings from the California delegation breakfast at the DNC where before he had a cup of coffee Democratic Party Chair John Burton—much like his old pal Guv Jerry Brown once did—just compared the Republicans to Nazi propagandist Joseph Goebbels, for "telling the big lie," a reference to several [putative] falsehoods GOP VP nominee Paul Ryan recently told.
>
> "They lie and they don't care if people think they lie ... Joseph Goebbels—it's the big lie, you keep repeating it," Burton said Monday before the Blake Hotel breakfast. He said Ryan told "a bold-faced lie and he doesn't care that it was a lie. That was Goebbels, the big lie."

You see the progression. Journalists claiming to be engaged in "fact checking" make tendentious arguments against Republicans. Left-wing partisans rely on the authority of the "fact checkers" to call their opponents liars or even Nazis.

A Sense of Desperation

One gets a sense of desperation from both the Democrats, who are trying to reelect a president with a lousy record, and the MSM, who are trying to restore the authority they enjoyed when they aspired to objectivity, or at least pretended convincingly to do so.

Obama may yet eke out an ugly victory, but the decline of the MSM's authority seems inexorable. And it's not only "fact checkers" who are acting like out-and-out partisans. *Time*'s Joe Klein is "the Pope of American political journalists" according to the French newspaper *Le Nouvel Observateur*. Real-

ClearPolitics notes an ex cathedra [infallible] pronouncement he made the other day when he granted an audience to the *New York Times*'s Helene Cooper:

> Cooper: Four years of covering Barack Obama, he does not play the race card. Not in a negative way. He does not do that.
>
> Klein: He hates it. He hates it. He probably should, though. He probably should address it because the bitterness out there is really becoming marked.

Some may dispute Cooper's claim that Obama doesn't "play the race card." But Klein's assertion that he "probably should" is really quite stunning. It's almost certainly bad advice. Indeed, we'd say following it in 2008 would have been one of the few ways he could have lost to John McCain. Successful or not, the attempt to foment racial division would be as repugnant coming from a black leftist as from a white conservative.

Above all, though: What in the world is a journalist doing offering such rancid advice? In general terms, the same thing all those "fact checkers" are doing. Also the same thing journalists did when they slandered the Tea Party as racist, and when they wrote puff pieces about ObamaCare and insisted the public would learn to love it, and when they falsely blamed conservatives for the Tucson massacre.

During the Obama era, so-called mainstream journalism has increasingly been characterized by a blurring of the distinction between not only fact and opinion but opinion and propaganda. One can only hope the audience sees matters more clearly.

| *"The mutual-aggression pacts that govern politics make futile the fact-checking machinations of journalists."*

News Media Fact-Checking Is Futile

Jack Shafer

Jack Shafer is a blogger and columnist for Reuters news service. In the following viewpoint, he maintains that the growth of the fact-checking industry has led to a greater sensitivity to political lies. Shafer argues that although it may be necessary to document and challenge misleading and inaccurate statements, it is largely futile. Politicians, he says, will continue to lie because it is effective—it appeals to certain demographics and will motivate some voters to get out and vote. He asserts that as long as political lies confirm their preconceived beliefs, many voters will be okay with it. In addition, he maintains, it behooves some candidates to ignore or reject the judgments of fact-checkers, because the latter are viewed as part of the biased mainstream media.

As you read, consider the following questions:

1. Which fact-checking site does Shafer call "the grand-daddy"?

2. According to the author, what politician unveiled a scurrilous attack ad on Mitt Romney in 2008 and then vowed not to air it?

3. What does Brooks Jackson, as cited by Shafer, think about how political campaigns have come to perceive fact-checking operations?

If you've kept your shirt dry while canoeing the rivers of our current presidential campaign, it's likely that you've been skilled enough to avoid the logjams and snags of "dishonesty" and "lies" that the parties and press have flung into the water. While it's true that politicians and their campaigns and their ads routinely lie—I hear no disagreement on that point, so I'll continue—never have politicians and the press expressed such indignation at campaign exaggerations, fibs and falsehoods.

For example, after Representative Paul Ryan (R-Wisc.) gave his acceptance speech this week at the Republican National Convention, the press corps fact-checkers instantly took hammers and tweezers to his address. "The Most Dishonest Convention Speech . . . Ever?" asked Jonathan Cohn in the liberal *New Republic*, but the non-partisan press accused Ryan of having misled listeners and taken "factual shortcuts," too. *The Week* counted up the 15 euphemisms for "lying" the press (partisan and non-partisan) used to describe the speech.

The Fact-Checking Industry

I suspect the growing sensitivity to political lies has less to do with more lying by more politicians than it does with the growth of the fact-checking industry over the last decade or so. Every campaign speech, big or small, every campaign ad, local or national, every fund-raising letter is fodder for the modern fact-checkers, who have multiplied in the pages of our newspapers like termites in breeding season: FactCheck.org (the granddaddy of these sites, from the Annenberg Public Policy Center, which got started in the mid-2000s) and the

later arrivals PolitiFact (*Tampa Bay Times*), The Fact Checker (*Washington Post*), AP Fact Check (Associated Press) and CNN Fact Check, all of which run regular fact checks. Other news organizations muster ad hoc journalistic militias to grade the truth-value of political speech. Today's [August 31, 2012,] *New York Times* piece, "Facts Take a Beating in Acceptance Speeches," does that for the Republican National Convention.

As much as I applaud the fact-checker profession—it's vital for politicians to know that we know that they know they're lying—the enterprise is a mug's game. Of course politicians and their campaigns lie. Of course they continue to lie even when called out. If you think otherwise, you're looking for truth in all the wrong places.

Bending the Truth

Politicians engage in deliberative rhetoric on the stump, in legislative speeches and in campaign commercials. Their primary goal is to convince audiences that their positions are right, and persuade them to vote, make campaign donations, echo their support, recruit additional supporters or take some other action. Truth-telling would matter a lot more to politicians if it were as effective in persuading people as truth-bending. Plus, trapping the truth and serving it in a palatable form to an audience is damn hard, as any university professor can tell you. It's easier and more effective for campaigns to trim, spice and cook facts to serve something tastier, even if they must brawl with the fact-checkers in the aftermath.

You might as well fact-check a sermon as fact-check a campaign speech. Neither are exercises in finding the truth. That doesn't mean we can excuse political lies. Please take a mallet to Romney's fallacious assertion that Obama ended work requirements for welfare and to the Obama campaign's ad that misstated Romney's views on abortion. I pair these two fact checks not just to declare moral equivalence between the two parties or candidates but to demonstrate that the mutual-aggression pacts that govern politics make futile the fact-checking machinations of journalists. Give them a million billion Pinocchios [ratings for untruthfulness] and they'll still not behave. Remember, the Republican-on-Republican fact-action was hairier during the primaries, when more desperate candidates were in the race. See also the 2008 Democratic Party and Republican Party campaigns for presidential nominations, when most of the candidates were eager to say the least defensible things about their fellow party members if that gave them a better shot at the ticket. Like in 2008, when Mike Huckabee unveiled to the press a scurrilous 30-second attack ad calling Mitt Romney too dishonest to be president, but then, as a statement against gutter politics, vowed not to air it.

The Role of Journalists

Journalists, even of the fact-checking variety, like to imagine they're in the grandstands, watching and commenting on the action, when they're actually part of the game. As the *Washington Post* reports today, far from deploring the process, the candidates enjoying gaming the fact-checkers to their advantage. "The Obama campaign has tasked one media officer to deal exclusively with fact checkers' questions, and top Romney adviser Eric Fehrnstrom often personally handles requests," says the piece. Brooks Jackson, FactCheck.org director, who produced fact-check journalism for CNN during the 1992 presidential election, expresses his worries that campaigns have come to regard their head-butting with fact-checkers as a kind of badge of honor. It's like raising a naughty kid who enjoys time-outs.

Fact-checking, explains the *Post*, is not for politicians but for voters. I suppose fact-checking would matter more to voters if they expected honesty from their politicians. But most don't. Instead of vetted policy lectures, voters crave rhetoric that stirs their unfact-checked hearts. As long as the deception is honest, pointing in the direction they want to go, they're all right with it.

> "Media fact-checking operations aren't about checking facts so much as they are about a rearguard action to keep inconvenient truths out of the conversation."

News Media Fact-Checking Is a Tool to Control Public Discourse

Mark Hemingway

Mark Hemingway is a political columnist and online editor of the Weekly Standard. *In the following viewpoint, he views the growth of the fact-checking industry as a reaction to the explosion of emerging online media outlets and mobile technology in recent years. Hemingway asserts that fact-checking allows the mainstream media to control discourse by routinely imposing their own opinions on their readers and dismissing the opinion of conservatives. In addition, the media seem oblivious to the distinction between fact and opinion. Because the media establishment has deemed fact-checking to be a noble and worthwhile pursuit, there has been little analysis of how well they have been doing their job until recently. Hemingway predicts that that trend will continue, and fact-checkers will continue to be less of an objective referee than a biased participant in political media coverage.*

As you read, consider the following questions:

1. As stated by Hemingway, in what year was PolitiFact launched?

2. According to the author, where are five of the richest counties in America located?

3. What were the findings of a Smart Politics content analysis of 500 PolitiFact stories from January 2010 to January 2011, as reported by Hemingway?

If you've ever found yourself engaged in a futile, one-sided argument with a politician on your TV screen, you're hardly alone in your frustration. However, if you're inclined to jot down such intemperate outbursts, and have the chutzpah [brazenness] to charge people for your services—you might have what it takes to join the ranks of one of journalism's most popular and elite new breeds.

Today's Fact-Checking Operations

They call themselves "fact checkers," and with the name comes a veneer of objectivity doubling as a license to go after any remark by a public figure they find disagreeable for any reason. Just look at the Associated Press [AP] to understand how the scheme works. The venerable wire service's recent "fact check" of statements made at the November 12 [2011] GOP [Republican] presidential candidates' foreign policy debate was a doozy. Throwing no less than seven reporters at the effort, the piece came up with some unusual examples of what it means to correct verifiable truths.

On Iran, former Massachusetts governor Mitt Romney suggested that the U.S. government should make it "very clear that the United States of America is willing, in the final analysis, if necessary, to take military action to keep Iran from having a nuclear weapon."

Little did Romney realize that the AP is the final arbiter of America's tactical military capabilities and can say with certainty that a military attack on Iran's nuclear program should not be attempted: "The U.S. certainly has military force readily at hand to destroy Iran's known nuclear development sites in short order. This is highly unlikely, however, because of the strategic calculation that an attack would be counterproductive and ultimately ineffective, spawning retaliation against U.S. allies and forces in the region, and merely delaying eventual nuclear weapons development."

Also fortunate for the savvy news consumer, the AP apparently has a better grasp of what America's intelligence agencies do and do not know than [debate participant] Newt Gingrich, a man who used to be third in line for the presidency [i.e., Speaker of the House] and has received countless classified intelligence briefings.

Fact-Checking Opinions

At the debate, Gingrich suggested that there was room for improvement at America's intelligence agencies, and noted in particular that we don't have a reliable intelligence operation in Pakistan. The AP sprang to the defense of the CIA:

"The U.S. killing of a succession of al Qaeda figures in Pakistan, none more prized by America than Osama bin Laden, demonstrates that the United States indeed gets vital and reliable intelligence out of Pakistan. While it may have been true when Gingrich left government in 1999 that the CIA's spy network was limited, since 2001 the agency has dramatically expanded its on-the-ground operations worldwide," the AP "fact check" concluded.

The fact that bin Laden, the most wanted man on the planet, was living in a compound in Pakistan possibly for years may seem like a sign that our intelligence sources in the country leave something to be desired—but guess again, Newt.

If these examples are laughably transparent attempts by the AP to weigh in with its own opinions against the opinions of the GOP candidates—thinly disguised as "fact checking"— they're not unusual. And the rare occasions where fact checkers deign to deal with actual facts and figures inspire little more confidence.

PolitiFact

Media fact checking endeavors have never been more popular and influential than they are now, largely thanks to the success of the *St. Petersburg Times* feature called "PolitiFact." Launched in 2007, PolitiFact purports to judge the factual accuracy of statements from politicians and other prominent national figures.

A statement is presented in bold type at the top of the page, usually accompanied by a picture of the speaker. Off to the side is a "Truth-O-Meter" graphic depicting an old-school instrument gauge. The Truth-O-Meter displays a red, yellow, or green light depending on whether the statement is rated "true," "mostly true," "half true," "mostly false," "false," or "pants on fire!" (To drive the point home, on the website the "pants on fire!" rating is accompanied by animated flames.) Below the Truth-O-Meter is a short explanation from PolitiFact's editors justifying their rating.

The feature quickly gained popularity, and in 2009 the *St. Petersburg Times* won a Pulitzer Prize for PolitiFact, endowing the innovation with a great deal of credibility. "According to the Pulitzer Prize–winning PolitiFact . . ." has now become a kind of Beltway Tourette syndrome, a phrase sputtered by journalists and politicians alike in an attempt to buttress their arguments.

If the stated goal seems simple enough—providing an impartial referee to help readers sort out acrimonious and hyperbolic political disputes—in practice PolitiFact does nothing of the sort.

The Failure of PolitiFact

Here's a not-atypical case study. On November 7, 2010, newly elected Senator Rand Paul appeared on ABC's *This Week with Christiane Amanpour*. One of the topics of discussion was pay for federal workers. "The average federal employee makes $120,000 a year," Paul said. "The average private employee makes $60,000 a year."

Given that the news these days often boils down to debates over byzantine [archaic and convoluted] policy details, Paul's statement is about as close to an empirically verifiable fact as you're likely to hear a politician utter.

And the numbers are reasonably clear. According to the latest data from the Bureau of Economic Analysis [BEA]—yes, that's a government agency—federal workers earned average pay and benefits of $123,049 in 2009 while private workers made on average $61,051 in total compensation. What's more, the pay gap between the federal and private sectors has been growing substantially. A decade ago, average pay and benefits for federal workers was $76,187—federal civil servants have seen a 62 percent increase in their compensation since then, more than double the 30.5 percent increase in the private sector.

So federal workers are paid twice as much and their income has been rising over twice as fast. If that's not outrageous enough, from December 2007 to June 2009, the federal workforce saw a 46 percent increase in the number of employees with salaries over $100,000, a 119 percent increase in the number of those making over $150,000, and a 93 percent increase in the number of federal civil servants making over $170,000. Note that these figures do not include benefits, overtime, or bonuses.

Not only that, during Obama's first two years in office, while the unemployment rate hovered near or above double digits, the size of the federal workforce increased by 7 percent. The president called for a federal pay freeze at the end of 2010; however, under the president's supposed pay freeze, 1.1 million civil servants—the majority of the federal workforce— are still slated to get $2.5 billion in pay increases. And with the country on the verge of recession (again), 5 of the richest counties in America now surround Washington, D.C. Given who the largest employer in the area is, this is hardly surprising.

Not only is what Senator Paul said about federal pay verifiably true, his simple recitation of the most basic facts of the matter doesn't even begin to illustrate the extent of the problem.

A Problematic Rating

Yet PolitiFact rated Senator Paul's statement "false." According to PolitiFact's editors, because Paul did not explicitly say the figures he was citing include pay and benefits, he was being misleading. The average reader would assume he was only talking about salary. "BEA found that federal civilian employees earned $81,258 in salary, compared to $50,464 for private-sector workers. That cuts the federal pay advantage almost exactly in half, to nearly $31,000," writes PolitiFact.

So the average federal employee makes a mere $31,000 more a year in salary than the average private sector worker— but also gets a benefits package worth four times what the average private sector worker gets.

PolitiFact further muddies the waters by suggesting that the discrepancy between public and private sector averages isn't an apples-to-apples comparison. Again, Andrew Biggs, the former Social Security Administration deputy commissioner for policy, and Jason Richwine of the Center for Data Analysis, writing in these pages ("Yes, They're Overpaid: The Truth About Federal Workers' Compensation," *The Weekly Standard*, February 14, 2011), observed that the most favorable studies of federal worker compensation "controlling for age, education, experience, race, gender, marital status, immigration status, state of residence, and so on" still find federal workers are overpaid by as much as 22 percent.

What accounts for PolitiFact's inexplicably obtuse explanation? If you suspect that it might be PolitiFact's pants that are on fire, you're not alone.

The Growth of Fact-Checking

PolitiFact and the Associated Press are hardly the only outfits playing this game. In recent years, the *Washington Post* and other media outlets have dutifully followed in PolitiFact's footsteps and launched "fact checking" features, while established organizations such as the Annenberg Public Policy Center's FactCheck.org have gained increased prominence.

It's true that these items are popular. Who doesn't want to use the "facts" as a cudgel against his political opponents? Groups across the political spectrum are increasingly prone to sending out press releases crowing about the latest media "fact check" finding that happens to vindicate their particular views.

But it seems the most outspoken fans of media fact-checking operations come from within the media themselves. "Has anyone else noticed that the Associated Press has been doing some strong fact-checking work lately, aggressively debunking all kinds of nonsense, in an authoritative way, without any of the usual he-said-she-said crap that often mars political reporting?" *Washington Post* blogger Greg Sargent wrote last year [2010].

The Elena Kagan Case

Sargent was conducting a fawning interview with the AP's Washington bureau chief Ron Fournier about the outlet's fact-checking operation. "The AP, for instance, definitively knocked down claims that [Supreme Court Justice] Elena Kagan is an 'ivory tower peacenik,'" Sargent wrote.

Not surprisingly, Fournier agreed with Sargent. "What we tend to forget in journalism is that we got in the business to check facts," Fournier says. "Not just to tell people what Obama said and what Gingrich said. It is groundless to say that Kagan is antimilitary. So why not call it groundless? This is badly needed when people are being flooded with information."

Sargent and Fournier's ouroboros [circularity] of self-congratulation inadvertently revealed a problem: When it comes to fact checking, the media seem oblivious to the distinction between verifying facts and passing judgment on opinions they personally find disagreeable.

Again, here are the facts: Kagan was a dean at a law school that had banned ROTC [a college-level military training program] over what she referred to as the military's "repugnant" ban on openly gay service. This was, not surprisingly, an issue raised when she was nominated for her current position on the Supreme Court. The AP's own fact check even noted that she filed a legal brief in support of colleges that wanted to uphold their policies restricting military recruiters on campus, though she opted not to join the lawsuit. Whether the fact that Kagan valued making a statement about gay rights over supporting the vital national security effort of military recruitment amounts to being "antimilitary" is quite obviously a matter of opinion, as is the charge that she's an "ivory tower peacenik."

Revealingly, the inflammatory phrase "ivory tower peacenik" was never actually used by Kagan's critics—it was from the AP headline and the first sentence of its fact check:

"Elena Kagan is no ivory-tower peacenik." Here the AP pulled off a seriously impressive feat of yellow journalism [reporting sensationalist items rather than researched facts to sell papers]. By caricaturing the tone of the actual criticisms, the AP set up a straw man [misrepresentation] for its "fact check" to knock down before the reader even got past the headline.

Rating Opinions

At the most basic level, the media's new "fact checkers" remain obdurately unwilling to let opinions simply be opinions. Earlier this year the AP fact checked a column by former GOP presidential candidate Tim Pawlenty in which the former Minnesota governor asserted that "Obamacare is unconstitutional." Contra Pawlenty, the AP intoned, "Obama's health care overhaul might be unconstitutional in Pawlenty's opinion, but it is not in fact unless the Supreme Court says so."

The AP aligns itself here with the myth of judicial supremacy, namely the mistaken idea that the Supreme Court has a monopoly on deciding what is and is not constitutional. But aside from this amateur-hour excursion into legal theory, the AP betrays a more basic problem of reading comprehension: Pawlenty's *USA Today* column appeared in a section of the newspaper clearly labeled OPINION in large, bold letters.

And when you take the media's desire to tamp down opinions they don't like to its logical extreme, things get really messy. Sometimes opinions multiply to the point that media gatekeepers can no longer contain them. Thus "narratives" are born, which are even more pernicious to "fact checkers" than opinions.

"The AP also did an extensive investigation into Obama's handling of the Gulf [oil] spill [in April 2010], and concluded it 'shows little resemblance to [Hurricane] Katrina,'" writes Sargent. "As [liberal *Washington Monthly* blogger] Steve Benen noted in lauding this effort, the AP definitively debunked a key media narrative as 'baseless.'"

One could ask whether the BP oil spill was being compared with Katrina simply because of its relative proximity and public opinion that the Obama administration handled the crisis similarly poorly. But why bother? The very idea of fact checking a broad comparison should send readers who give a damn about facts screaming for the exits.

The Role of Journalism

While it was always difficult in practice, once upon a time journalists at least paid obeisance to the idea of reporting the facts, as opposed to commenting on "narratives"—let alone being responsible for creating and debunking them.

But today's fact checkers are largely uninterested in emphasizing the primacy of information. Accordingly, this is what happens when the media talk about fact checking: The *Washington Post* pats the AP on the back for questioning the veracity of a media-created narrative ex post facto [after the fact], then cites a brazenly partisan blogger as proof that the effort to smack it down was successful.

What's going on here should be obvious enough. With the rise of cable news and the Internet, traditional media institutions are increasingly unable to control what political rhetoric and which narratives catch fire with the public. Media fact-checking operations aren't about checking facts so much as they are about a rearguard action to keep inconvenient truths out of the conversation.

Blatant Bias

While there's been little examination of the broader phenomenon of media fact checking, the University of Minnesota Humphrey School of Public Affairs recently took a close look at PolitiFact. Here's what they found:

A Smart Politics content analysis of more than 500 Politi-Fact stories from January 2010 through January 2011 finds that current and former Republican officeholders have been assigned substantially harsher grades by the news organization than their Democratic counterparts. In total, 74 of the 98 statements by political figures judged "false" or "pants on fire" over the last 13 months were given to Republicans, or 76 percent, compared to just 22 statements for Democrats (22 percent).

You can believe that Republicans lie more than three times as often as Democrats. Or you can believe that, at a minimum, PolitiFact is engaging in a great deal of selection bias, to say nothing of pushing tendentious arguments of its own.

The media establishment has largely rallied round the self-satisfied consensus that fact checking is a noble pursuit. Nonetheless there are signs of an impending crack-up. In their rush to hop on the fact-checking bandwagon, the media appear to have given little thought to what their new obsession says about how well or poorly they perform their jobs.

It's impossible for the media to fact check without rendering judgment on their own failures. Seeing the words "fact check" in a headline plants the idea in the reader's mind that it's something out of the ordinary for journalists to check facts. Shouldn't that be an everyday part of their jobs that goes without saying? And if they aren't normally checking facts, what exactly is it that they're doing?

As such, fact checking frequently involves one news organization publicly accusing competing organizations of malpractice. Instead of newsroom watercooler kvetching [griping] and burying subtle digs in the eleventh paragraph, friendly fire is breaking out into the open.

The Effects of Fact-Checking

Influential *Politico* blogger/reporter Ben Smith is one of the few media voices sounding the alarm about the pitfalls of fact checking. "At their worst, they're doing opinion journalism under pseudo-scientific banners, something that's really corrosive to actual journalism, which if it's any good is about reported fact in the first place," Smith observes.

When he wrote that, Smith was quite rightly annoyed with Glenn Kessler, who writes "The Fact Checker" blog on the *Washington Post* website. (Kessler's gimmick is rating political statements on a scale of one to four with cutesy Pinocchio-nose graphics.)

On August 17 [2011], Kessler wrote an item supporting President Obama's denial at a town hall in Iowa that Vice President Joe Biden had called Tea Party activists "terrorists" in a meeting with congressional Democrats. In the process, Kessler had singled out *Politico* for breaking the story.

Politico's, report about Biden's comments indeed created a minor controversy. Days later, the vice president came forward and claimed the report was "absolutely not true," that he was merely engaged in a discussion with unnamed lawmakers who were venting about the Tea Party.

After supplying a rudimentary summary of what happened, Kessler reached a conclusion that is at once unsure of itself and sharply judgmental. "Frankly, we are dubious that Biden actually said this. And if he did, he was simply echoing what another speaker said, in a private conversation, as opposed to making a public statement."

In response, Smith unloaded on Kessler. "Either [Biden] said it, or he didn't. That's the fact to check here. The way to check it is to report it out, not to attack the people who did report it out and label their reporting 'dubious' based on nothing more than instinct and the questionable and utterly self-interested word of politicians and their staffers."

Provoked by Kessler, *Politico* took the unusual step of actually detailing how the Biden story was nailed down. *Politico* maintains that Biden's remarks were confirmed by five different sources in the room with Biden, and that they were in contact with the vice president's office for hours before the story ran. Biden's office had ample opportunity to answer the reporters' account before it ran and didn't dispute it.

Note that despite Biden's subsequent denials, the vice president's office never asked for a formal retraction. The facts here seem to suggest that the vice president, whose history of plagiarism and verbal incontinence is the stuff of legend, not only called Tea Partiers "terrorists" but later lied about having done so. One would think that this would be a news story in itself.

But instead of looking at these facts, it appears Glenn Kessler engaged in what his colleague Greg Sargent referred to as all "the usual he-said-she-said crap that often mars political reporting"—but with the extra dollop of sanctimony that comes from writing under the "pseudo-scientific banner" of "The Fact Checker."

Evaluating Fact-Checking Operations

Of course, Ben Smith's apostasy is born of experience. Even before the dustup between the *Washington Post* and *Politico* he found his own reporting being dissected, unfairly in his view, by an AP fact check back in May [2011].

After that experience he concluded that while fact checking can be useful, "Most political disputes are too nuanced to fit the 'fact check' framework." As more well-intentioned reporters get sandbagged by "fact checkers," perhaps Smith won't be alone in venting this view publicly.

In the meantime, don't get your hopes up that Smith's journalistic peers will be receptive to his criticisms. A major reason PolitiFact kicked off a national fact-checking craze was that it was introduced in 2007, just in time to play a major role in the last presidential election, in which one contender was an overwhelming media favorite. (Brooks Jackson, the founder of FactCheck.org, actually traces the genesis of media fact checking to the frustration journalists felt over the supposedly unfair media coverage Michael Dukakis received in the 1988 campaign. And who has not lamented the unflattering media coverage Democrats have received since then?)

Like it or not, it seems that media "fact checks" are poised to be even more widespread in the coming election. Aside from fact-checking debates afterward, as the Associated Press has done, the *Washington Post* and *Bloomberg*, which hosted the October 11 GOP debate, actually took the novel tack of running "fact checks" on what the candidates were saying in real time. While presidential candidates should not be above being held accountable for what they say in such a forum, there is good reason to be skeptical that instantaneous evaluations will ever prove useful or fair.

So with 2012 just around the corner, brace yourself for a fact-checking deluge. Just remember: The fact checker is less often a referee than a fan with a rooting interest in the outcome.

> *"The failure of our electronic media to inform the public about centrally important global developments is itself a security threat to the republic."*

The News Media Must Do a Better Job of Informing the Public of Vital Global Developments

Juan Cole

Juan Cole is a blogger, author, and professor of history and the director of the Center for South Asian Studies at the University of Michigan. In the following viewpoint, he notes that the US media barely covered the 2010 floods in Pakistan, which displaced millions of people, submerged entire cities, destroyed crops and infrastructure, and threatened the country's security. Cole suggests that there are several explanations for the lack of media coverage: there was a general lack of interest among the US public; the Pakistani disaster did not play into US domestic politics, which views Pakistan as an Islamic country that holds anti-American attitudes; and adequate media coverage would be expensive and logistically challenging for US corporate media. Cole argues that the media's failure to inform the public about key global developments threatens public security.

As you read, consider the following questions:

1. According to Cole, how many Pakistanis were displaced by the 2010 floods?

2. What city in Pakistan was submerged by flood waters on August 30, as reported by the author?

3. How many people does Cole say live in Pakistan?

The Great Deluge in Pakistan passed almost unnoticed in the United States despite President Obama's repeated assertions that the country is central to American security. Now, with new evacuations and flooding afflicting Sindh Province and the long-term crisis only beginning in Pakistan, it has washed almost completely off American television and out of popular consciousness.

Media Failure

Don't think we haven't been here before. In the late 1990s, the American mass media could seldom be bothered to report on the growing threat of al-Qaeda. In 2002, it slavishly parroted White House propaganda about Iraq, helping prepare the way for a senseless war. No one yet knows just what kind of long-term instability the Pakistani floods are likely to create, but count on one thing: the implications for the United States are likely to be significant and by the time anyone here pays much attention, it will already be too late.

Few Americans were shown—by the media conglomerates of their choice—the heartbreaking scenes of eight million Pakistanis displaced into tent cities, of the submerging of a string of mid-sized cities (each nearly the size of New Orleans), of vast areas of crops ruined, of infrastructure swept away, damaged, or devastated at an almost unimaginable level, of futures destroyed, and opportunistic Taliban bombings continuing. The boiling disgust of the Pakistani public with the incompetence, insouciance, and cupidity of their corrupt ruling class is little appreciated.

The likely tie-in of these floods (of a sort no one in Pakistan had ever experienced) with global warming was seldom mentioned. Unlike, say, BBC Radio, corporate television did not tell the small stories—of, for instance, the female sharecropper who typically has no rights to the now-flooded land on which she grew now-ruined crops thanks to a loan from an estate-owner, and who is now penniless, deeply in debt, and perhaps permanently excluded from the land. That one of the biggest stories of the past decade could have been mostly blown off by television news and studiously ignored by the American public is a further demonstration that there is something profoundly wrong with corporate news-for-profit. (The print press was better at covering the crisis, as was publically-supported radio, including the BBC and National Public Radio.)

The Importance of Pakistan

In his speech on the withdrawal of designated combat units from Iraq last week [early September, 2010], Barack Obama put Pakistan front and center in American security doctrine, "But we must never lose sight of what's at stake. As we speak, al-Qaeda continues to plot against us, and its leadership remains anchored in the border regions of Afghanistan and Pakistan." Even if Pakistan were not a major non-NATO ally of the United States, it is the world's sixth most populous country and the 44th largest economy, according to the World Bank. The flooding witnessed in the Indus Valley is unprecedented in the country's modern history and was caused by a combination of increasingly warm ocean water and a mysterious blockage of the jet stream, which drew warm, water-laden air north to Pakistan, over which it burst in sheets of raging liquid. If the floods that followed prove a harbinger of things to come, then they are a milestone in our experience of global warming, a big story in its own right.

News junkies who watch a lot of television broadcasts could not help but notice with puzzlement that as the cosmic catastrophe unfolded in Pakistan, it was nearly invisible on American networks. I did a LexisNexis [an online publications index] search for the terms "Pakistan" and "flood" in broadcast transcripts (covering mostly American networks) from July 31st to September 4th, [2010,] and it returned only about 1,100 hits. A search for the name of troubled actress Lindsay Lohan returned 653 search results in the same period and one for "Iraq," more than 3,000 hits (the most the search engine will count). A search for "mosque" and "New York" yielded 1,300 hits. Put another way, the American media, whipped into an artificial frenzy by anti-Muslim bigots like New York gubernatorial candidate Rick Lazio and GOP [Republican] hatemonger Newt Gingrich, were far more interested in the possible construction of a Muslim-owned interfaith community center two long blocks from the old World Trade Center site than in the sight of millions of hapless Pakistani flood victims.

The Global Warming Angle

Of course, some television correspondents did good work trying to cover the calamity, including CNN's Reza Sayah and Sanjay Gupta, but they generally got limited air time and poor time slots. (Gupta's special report on the Pakistan floods aired the evening of September 5th, the Sunday before Labor Day, not exactly a time when most viewers might be expected to watch hard news.) As for the global warming angle, it was not completely ignored. On August 13th, reporter Dan Harris interviewed NASA [National Aeronautics and Space Administration] scientist Gavin Schmidt on ABC's "Good Morning America" show at 7:45 am. The subject was whether global warming could be the likely cause for the Pakistan floods and other extreme weather events of the summer, with Schmidt pointing out that such weather-driven cataclysms are going to become more common later in the twenty-first century. Becky Anderson at CNN did a similar segment at 4 pm on August 16th. My own search of news transcripts suggests that that was about it for commercial television.

Disaster Almost Unknown by Americans

It's worth reviewing the events that most Americans hardly know happened:

The deluge began on July 31st, when heavier than usual monsoon rains caused mudslides in the northwest of Pakistan. Within two days, the rapidly rising waters had already killed 800 people. On August 2nd, the United Nations announced that about a million people had been driven from their homes. Among the affected areas was the Swat Valley, already suffering from large numbers of refugees and significant damage from an army offensive against the Pakistani Taliban in the spring-summer of 2009. In the district of Dera Ismail Khan alone, hundreds of villages were destroyed by the floods, forcing shelterless villagers to sleep on nearby raised highways.

The suddenly homeless waited in vain for the government to begin to deliver aid, as public criticism of President Asaf Ali Zardari and Prime Minister Yousuf Raza Gilani surged. President Zardari's opulent trip to France and Britain (during which he visited his chateau in Normandy) at this moment of national crisis was pilloried. On August 8th in Birmingham, England, a furious Pakistani-British man threw both his shoes at him, repeating a famously humiliating incident in which an Iraqi journalist threw a shoe at President George W. Bush. Fearing the response in Pakistan, the president's Pakistan People's Party attempted to censor the video of the incident, and media offices in that country were closed down or sometimes violently attacked if they insisted on covering it. Few or no American broadcast outlets appear to have so much as mentioned the incident, though it pointed to the increasing dissatisfaction of Pakistanis with their elected government.

(The army has gotten better marks for its efficient aid work, raising fears that some ambitious officers could try to parlay a newfound popularity into yet another in the country's history of military coups.)

A Worsening Situation

By August 5th, the floods had taken an estimated 1,600 lives, though some aid officials complained (and would continue to do so) that the death toll was far larger than reported. Unlike the Haitian earthquake or the BP oil spill in the Gulf of Mexico, this still-building and far more expansive disaster was initially greeted by the world community with a yawn. The following day, the government evacuated another half-million people as the waters headed toward southern Punjab. At that point, some 12 million Pakistanis had been adversely affected in some way. On August 7th, as the waters advanced on the southernmost province, Sindh, through some of the country's richest farmlands just before harvest time, another million people were evacuated. Prime Minister Gilani finally paid his first visit to some of the flood-stricken regions.

By August 9th, nearly 14 million people had been affected by the deluge, the likes of which had never been experienced in the region in modern history, and at least 20% of the country was under water. At that point, in terms of its human impact, the catastrophe had already outstripped both the 2004 tsunami and the 2010 Haiti earthquake. On August 10th, the United Nations announced that six million Pakistanis needed immediate humanitarian aid just to stay alive.

On August 14th, another half-million people were evacuated from the Sindhi city of Jacobabad. By now, conspiracy theories were swirling inside Pakistan about landlords who had deliberately cut levees to force the waters away from their estates and into peasant villages, or about the possibility that the U.S. military had diverted the waters from its base at Jacobabad. It was announced that 18 million Pakistanis had now been adversely affected by the floods, having been displaced, cut off from help by the waters, or having lost crops, farms, and other property. The next day, U.N. Secretary-General Ban Ki-Moon, surveying the damage, pronounced it was "the worst disaster" he had ever seen.

More Misery

The following week a second crest of river water hit Sindh Province. On August 30th, it submerged the city of Sujawal (population 250,000). The next day, however, there were a mere 16 mentions of Pakistan on *all* American television news broadcasts, mostly on CNN. On Labor Day weekend, another major dam began to fail in Sindh and, by September 6th, several hundred thousand more people had to flee from Dadu district, with all but four districts in that rich agricultural province having seen at least some flooding.

Today, almost six million Pakistanis are still homeless, and many have not so much as received tents for shelter. In large swaths of the country, roads, bridges, crops, power plants—everything that matters to the economy—were inundated and damaged or simply swept away. Even if the money proves to be available for repairs (and that remains an open question), it will take years to rebuild what was lost and, for many among those millions, the future will mean nothing but immiseration, illness, and death.

Why the Floods Were Not News

In the United States, the contrast with the wall-to-wall cable news coverage of the Haitian earthquake in January [2010] and the consequent outpouring of public donations was palpable. Not only has the United Nations' plea for $460 million in aid to cover the first three months of flood response still not been met, but in the past week donations seem to have dried up. The U.S. government pledged $200 million (some diverted from an already planned aid program for Pakistan) and provided helicopter gunships to rescue cut-off refugees or ferry aid to them.

What of American civil society? No rock concerts were organized to help Pakistani children sleeping on highways or in open fields infested with vermin. No sports events offered receipts to aid victims at risk from cholera and other diseases. It was as if the great Pakistani deluge were happening in another dimension, beyond the ken of Americans.

A number of explanations have been offered for the lack of empathy, or even interest, not to speak of a visible American unwillingness to help millions of Pakistanis. As a start, there were perfectly reasonable fears, even among Pakistani-Americans, that such aid money might simply be pocketed by corrupt government officials. But was the Haitian government really so much more transparent and less corrupt than the Pakistani one?

Donor Fatigue

It has also been suggested that Americans suffer from donor fatigue, given the string of world disasters in recent years and the bad domestic economy. On August 16th, for instance, [conservative political commentator] Glenn Beck fulminated: "We can't keep spending. We are broke! Game over . . . no one is going to ride in to save you . . . You see the scene in Pakistan? People were waiting in line for aids [sic] from floods. And they were complaining, how come the aid is not here? Look, when America is gone, who's going to save the people in Pakistan? See, we got to change this one, because we're the ones that always ride in to save people."

Still, the submerging of a fifth of a country the size of Pakistan is—or at least should be—a dramatic global event and even small sums, if aggregated, would matter. (A dollar and a half from each American would have met the U.N. appeal.) Some have suggested that the Islamophobia visible in the de-

The History of Pakistan

The region of modern-day Pakistan has traces of civilization that date at least 5,000 years. The Mughal Empire flourished in the sixteenth and seventeenth centuries. The British dominated the region in the latter half of the nineteenth century. British India was partitioned into East Pakistan (which became Bangladesh in 1971), West Pakistan (modern-day Pakistan), and India in 1947. After gaining its independence, Pakistan experienced continual political turmoil under a series of military leaders. The constitution was suspended and restored or amended at least seven times in the period 1973–2007. General Pervez Musharraf came into power in 1999 after ousting the prime minster and declaring a state of emergency. In 2001, he declared himself to be president. His controversial rule as president ended with his resignation in August 2008, as the legislature threatened to begin impeachment proceedings against him on counts of gross misconduct and violations of the constitution. Musharaff soon went into exile in London. The September 2008 presidential elections were won by Asif Ali Zardari of the Pakistan People's Party (PPP).

Global Issues in Context, *"Pakistan,"* 2013.

bate about the Park 51 Muslim-owned community center in lower Manhattan left Americans far less willing to donate to Muslim disaster victims.

Pakistan and US National Security

And what of those national security arguments that nuclear-armed Pakistan is crucial not just to the American war in Afghanistan, but to the American way of life? Ironically, the collapse of the neoconservative narrative about what it takes to make the planet's "sole superpower" secure appears to have fallen on President Obama's head. One of the few themes he adopted wholeheartedly from the Bush administration has been the idea that a poor Asian country of 170 million halfway around the world, facing a challenge from a few thousand rural fundamentalists, is the key to the security of the United States.

If the Pakistani floods reveal one thing, it's that Americans now look on such explanations through increasingly jaundiced eyes. At the moment, no matter whether it's the Afghan War or those millions of desperate peasants and city dwellers in Pakistan, the public has largely decided to ignore the AfPak [Afghanistan-Pakistan] theater of operations. It's not so surprising. Having seen the collapse of our financial system at the hands of corrupt financiers produce mass unemployment and mass mortgage foreclosures, they have evidently decided, as even Glenn Beck admits, it's "game over" for imperial adventures abroad.

Another explanation may also bear some weight here, though you won't normally hear much about it. Was the decision of the corporate media not to cover the Pakistan disaster intensively a major factor in the public apathy that followed, especially since so many Americans get their news from television?

The Implications of Media Failure

The lack of coverage needs to be explained, since corporate media usually love apolitical, weather-induced disasters. But covering a flood in a distant Asian country is, for television, expensive and logistically challenging, which in these tough economic times may have influenced programming decisions. Obviously, there is as well a tendency in capitalist news to cover what will attract advertising dollars. Add to this the fact that, unlike the Iraq "withdrawal" story or the "mosque at

Ground Zero" controversy, the disaster in Pakistan was not a political football between the GOP and the Democratic Party. What if, in fact, Americans missed this calamity mostly because a bad news story set in a little-known South Asian country filled with Muslim peasants is not exactly [the TV hit drama] "Desperate Housewives" and couldn't hope to sell tampons, deodorant, or Cialis, or because it did not play into domestic partisan politics?

The great Pakistani deluge did not exist, it seems, because it was not on television, would not have delivered audiences to products, and was not all about us. As we saw on September 11, 2001, and again in March 2003, however, the failure of our electronic media to inform the public about centrally important global developments is itself a security threat to the republic.

> "Ride a bike off of a roof and smash to the ground and you can get your 15 minutes of fame as that video goes viral. Defend your nation or your faith and you are ignored or reviled."

The News Media Should Celebrate Traditional Values

Dan Gainor

Dan Gainor is a journalist, political columnist, and vice president of business and culture at the Media Research Center, a conservative media analysis organization. In the following viewpoint, he observes that the countercultural values that emerged in the 1960s—drug use, sexual promiscuity, a rejection of traditional values—are dominant in today's culture. Gainor blames the media for much of this shift, arguing that the media celebrates criminals, drug addicts, and sexual degenerates instead of true American heroes. For example, he states, the accomplishments of US military heroes are rarely covered in the mainstream news media. When they do deign to cover a hero, like the pro football quarterback Tim Tebow, Gainor maintains, it is to denigrate his religion and ridicule his high moral standards.

As you read, consider the following questions:

1. According to Gainor, what was said when the Americans triumphed in the Revolutionary War?

2. How many separate broadcasts did ABC, CBS, and NBC use to broadcast reports on Charlie Sheen's antics, according to the author?

3. In Gainor's opinion, what makes Tim Tebow a hero?

When Americans triumphed in the Revolutionary War, it was said that the world had turned upside down.

It has happened all over again 228 years later, except this time it's not the government that's changed, it's the culture. The 1960s ushered in counterculture in a big way. Long hair, psychedelic music, drugs and free love dominated the landscape for young people as many rebelled against traditional values.

The Victory of the Counterculture

But all that is as passé as Jackie Gleason in "The Honeymooners." In the eyes of the media, the counterculture won. As a society, we no longer celebrate the good things in America. The heroes of yesteryear are as hard to find as the use of the word "yesteryear." Valiant soldiers, astronauts, police officers and more have been torn down, criticized and destroyed by the keepers of our pop culture. Replacing them are street thug rappers, clueless athletes and brainless Hollywood stars.

America has been fighting wars in Afghanistan and Iraq for years. We've had 10 of our service people awarded the Congressional Medal of Honor. If you can name one of those recipients, you are probably a relative. How many Americans have heard of Lt. Michael P. Murphy and how he and his four-man SEAL [the US Navy's Sea, Air, and Land special forces] team fought 30 or 40 Taliban fighters. Murphy lost his life radioing for help for his men. Of the three broadcast networks, only NBC mentioned his heroism.

If only he'd been the star of a sleazy TV sitcom having a mid-life crisis reportedly involving drugs, living with two women (including one a former porn star) and getting fired [like] actor Charlie Sheen [who] was covered like he was actually somebody important. He's not. Still, ABC, CBS and NBC used 38 separate broadcasts to give viewers 4 hours, 51 minutes and 1 second of Sheen.

It's embarrassing that so-called journalists cared more about Sheen's "tiger blood" than the actual blood being shed by genuine heroes fighting in Iraq and Afghanistan. Gone are the days when a hero like WWII's Audie Murphy gets made into a huge action star. Instead, the best we can hope for is the feel-good story of wounded Iraq veteran J.R Martinez winning a mirror-ball trophy for his "Dancing With the Stars" victory.

As for astronauts, we've all but killed the manned space program. And police are now made to star in a 24-7 reality TV series on the Internet called Occupy Wall Street. There, no matter what they do, they are "pigs" and the Occupiers throw batteries, paint, even feces at the officers.

Who Are Today's Media Heroes?

Rappers, on the other hand, are beloved by TV, because they're "keeping it real." As real as mansions, limos and bottles of Cristal [an expensive champagne] can be, I guess. Rappers like 50 Cent or Kanye West are fixtures on news and entertainment shows as we wait for 50 Cent to bash another group on Twitter or Kanye to make another award show scene. Athletes are no better. Even in the midst of the NFL season, the NFLCrimes blog keeps busy with tales of arrest and even prison for top stars, presumably paid well enough to be able to stay out of jail for 17 weeks [of the NFL season].

The Tim Tebow Controversy

During Tebow's second season with the NFL, he was named starting quarterback of the Broncos and Kyle Orton was traded to the Kansas City Chiefs. Though Tebow garnered much attention for his ability to rush the ball and score touchdowns on his own, areas where he struggled were also highlighted—his passing abilities, or lack thereof when compared to other league quarterbacks. According to Dan Bickley of the *Arizona Republic*, "The scene is equally surreal in Denver, a city that once held impossibly high standards at quarterback, where a chorus line of successors attempted to emerge from the ever-present shadow of John Elway. And now the city is going bonkers over a quarterback who struggles to complete a simple forward pass?"

While many tuned in to see if Tebow would lead his team to the postseason with his shovel passes and handoffs, others changed channels when he continuously brought religion onto the field. After every touchdown or completed pass, he'd kneel down on one knee in short prayer. At the end of games, other players joined him in the middle of the field to pray. In interviews, Tebow was quick to talk about Jesus Christ and his love of God. Though thousands supported him, others began to view him as an annoyance.

On the radio, former NFL quarterback Jake Plummer stated, "I think he's a winner, and I respect that about him. I think that when he accepts the fact that we know that he loves Jesus Christ, then I think I'll like him even better. I don't hate him because of that. I just would rather not have to hear that every single time he takes a good snap or makes a good handoff."

Gale Biography in Context, *"Tim Tebow,"* 2013.

Every day brings new reminders that the more embarrass-ing your life, the more the tabloid news media will cover (or uncover) you. Many of the most familiar "star" names have so many stupid anecdotes, it's impossible to mention them all in one column. Lindsay Lohan, Britney Spears and Vanessa Hud-gens have all embarrassed themselves with inappropriate pho-tos. And they're all former Disney actresses. The D in "Dis-ney" must mean depraved.

But it's not like its Disney's fault. Hollywood produces more garbage every year and hides that fact with improved special effects and animation. Top films no longer even vaguely resemble real life or real people. We have wizards and super-heroes and toy cars. But few movies of anything even resem-bling real life.

Even the most essential parts of the family unit—hard-working fathers, understanding mothers and studious chil-dren—have become punch lines to a culture that celebrates the movie "Jackass" and daily chronicles of YouTube stupidity. Ride a bike off of a roof and smash to the ground and you can get your 15 minutes of fame as that video goes viral. De-fend your nation or your faith and you are ignored or reviled.

Tim Tebow

Denver Broncos [now New England Patriots] quarterback Tim Tebow's whole life is a miracle. Tim's mother Pam "contracted amoebic dysentery and the medicines used for her recovery threatened her unborn" child. She was urged to get an abor-tion and did not. Now, Tim is the starter for a team that was 1-4 when he took over. Since then, he's taken his team to a 6-5 record, just one game out of first place. He's done it with grit and determination, especially since his team traded their star receiver just days before he took over.

But despite that record of victory, Tebow is skewered by those who hate him, not for his success or even his team. No, they hate him for his Christian faith. Tebow has always been very public about that, giving to charity, professing his belief in God and even wearing Bible verses in the eye black beneath his eyes. Even former Broncos quarterback Jake Plummer took Tebow to task wanting him to be silent about his faith, saying, "when he accepts the fact that we know that he loves Jesus Christ, then I think I'll like him a little better."

For his part, Tebow isn't giving in, calling his "relationship with Jesus Christ" "the most important thing" in his life. Maybe he'll never be a great NFL quarterback or maybe he'll prove skeptics wrong and lead the Broncos to Super Bowl supremacy. That doesn't matter. Standing up for his faith. That's what makes Tim Tebow a hero—not football. He knows he'll be attacked for it because he is setting a standard and asking others to live up to it. And that doesn't stop him.

He's a rare reminder of what America used to be before the world turned upside down.

Periodical and Internet Sources Bibliography

The following articles have been selected to supplement the diverse views presented in this chapter.

Eric Alterman	"Let's Just Say It: The Republicans and the Media Are the Problem," *Nation*, August 13, 2012.
David Carr	"A Last Fact Check: It Didn't Work," *New York Times*, November 6, 2012.
Ross Douthat	"Fact-Checking Is Not Enough," *New York Times*, August 8, 2012.
Andrew Ferguson	"Is That a Fact-Check?," *Commentary*, October 2012.
Mike Gonzalez	"Checkers Confuse Facts with Opinions," *USA Today*, September 24, 2012.
Dan Kennedy	"PolitiFact and the Limits of Fact-Checking," *Huffington Post*, December 13, 2011. www.huffingtonpost.com.
Michael Moynihan	"2012 Presidential Campaign Said to Hit Unprecedented Level of Lying," *Daily Beast*, November 8, 2012. www.thedailybeast.com
Joseph Nistler	"Fact-Checking a Necessary Supplement to Modern Political Reporting, Panelists Say," Center for Journalism Ethics, April 24, 2012. http://ethics.journalism.wisc.edu.
Rem Rieder	"Truth-Squadding Mission," *American Journalism Review*, August 21, 2012.
Gabriel Rossman	"On Fact-Checking, Media Bias, and 'Nice Partitioning,'" *National Review*, August 30, 2012.
USA Today	"War on Election Fact-Checkers," September 24, 2012.

OPPOSING
VIEWPOINTS®
SERIES

| Are the News
Media Biased?

Chapter Preface

On November 6, 2012, Barack Obama was reelected to as US president. For many Republicans, the outcome was both a surprise and a disappointment. They had been confident that Mitt Romney, the Republican candidate, would pull off an upset. Much of the news media was predicting a much closer race than it was, and promoted polls that showed that the two candidates were in a real horserace. Some conservative-leaning polls even showed Romney with the potential to pull ahead in the final days. When the final results came in, it was a crushing blow to Romney supporters. In the weeks that followed President Obama's reelection, the Republican Party began to perform a postmortem on Romney's loss. One of the most frequently discussed reasons for President Obama's victory was the issue of liberal media bias.

Charges of liberal bias by conservatives in the media are not new. Many conservatives believe that the press tends to hold liberal beliefs and support Democratic legislation and policies. They argue that a liberal media bias is clear in the press's preference for Democratic politicians, a bias often revealed in fawning profiles of Democratic politicians or policy makers. During the 2012 presidential election, conservatives maintained that it was Barack Obama who received flattering media coverage, while Romney's every move was criticized or mocked. They complained that conservative ideas and policies were regularly painted as extremist and irresponsible while liberal policies were viewed as serious and effective. For many conservatives, it was time to take action against the liberal media's injustices.

A conservative media watchdog group, the Media Research Center (MRC), published an open letter signed by several major conservative leaders, including columnist and MRC founder Brent Bozell III, radio talk-show hosts Rush Limbaugh and Mark Levin, and activist Tony Perkins. "This election year, so much of the broadcast networks, their cable counterparts, and the major establishment print media are out of control with a deliberate and unmistakable leftist agenda," the letter read. It went on, "To put it bluntly: you are rigging this election and taking sides in order to pre-determine the outcome. In the quarter century since the Media Research Center was established to document liberal media bias, there has *never* been a more brazen and complete attempt by the liberal so-called 'news' media to decide the outcome of an election."

According to recent polls, many American share this view. In a Gallup poll published in September 2012, distrust of the mainstream media was at an all-time high. Gallup reported that 60 percent of Americans polled stated that they have "little or no trust in the mass media to report the news fully, accurately, and fairly."

Most of that negative perception came from Republicans, who had the least amount of trust in the media in general. Gallup concluded that

> Americans are clearly down on the news media this election year, with a record-high six in 10 expressing little or no trust in the mass media's ability to report the news fully, accurately, and fairly. This likely reflects the continuation of the trend seen in recent years, combined with the increased negativity toward the media that election years tend to bring. This is particularly consequential at a time when Americans need to rely on the media to learn about the platforms and perspectives of the two candidates vying to lead the country for the next four years.

The media's influence on the 2012 election is explored in the following chapter, which investigates the issue of news media bias. The viewpoints in the chapter debate liberal and conservative media bias, the impact of a partisan media on voters, the efficiency of government, and the possibility that charges of media bias could be used to manipulate the media.

> "The mainstream press . . . are a de facto arm of American liberalism."

The Dumbest Anchormen

Jonah Goldberg

Jonah Goldberg is an author, political columnist, and editor-at-large of the conservative magazine the National Review. *In the following viewpoint, he states that there is an obvious, long-standing liberal media bias that is so pervasive that it makes the mainstream press "a de facto arm of American liberalism." Goldberg contends that this bias was made clear in the 2012 presidential campaign, when reporters and fact-checkers took the side of President Obama against his conservative challengers and painted the Republican Party as a bunch of racists. He suggests that although American liberalism paints itself as logical and based in reality, it is in denial about the existence of a liberal bias in the media.*

As you read, consider the following questions:

1. According to Goldberg, what actor played Ron Burgundy in the movie *Anchorman*?

2. How many rounds of golf does Goldberg estimate that President Obama has played since he was elected?

3. What US politician does Goldberg identify as "the most prominent victim" of fact-checking during the 2012 presidential campaign?

"It's anchorman, not anchorlady—and that is a scientific fact!"

That's Champ Kind talking, a prominent member of the award-winning Channel 4 news team in the film *Anchorman*. While I might "earn" a "partly true" from the fact-checkers if I were to say the film was based on a true story, the reality is it's an absolutely ridiculous comedy that always makes me laugh. Set around a San Diego local-news show in the 1970s, *Anchorman* follows a male-chauvinist news team as it grapples with the turmoil that comes with admitting a female broadcaster into their midst.

But the plot's not really relevant for our purposes here. What brings the film to mind is one of the comic devices deployed from beginning to end: Everyone takes himself completely seriously even as he says the most ludicrously unserious things. All of the characters, led by Will Ferrell as Ron Burgundy (the anchorman referenced in the title), have no idea they're idiots and blowhards even as they boldly assert nakedly untrue or ridiculous things.

For instance, when the station manager explains that many of the affiliates have been "complaining about a lack of diversity on the news team," the staff is flummoxed.

"What in the hell's diversity?" Kind asks.

Ron Burgundy helpfully chimes in. "Well, I could be wrong, but I believe diversity is an old, old wooden ship that was used during the Civil War era." His colleagues nod like professors in the faculty lounge informed of the latest findings.

Later, when the team is coming unglued at the prospect that their boys' club will admit women, and Champ Kind is quoting the "scientific fact" that it is "anchorman, not anchorlady," another colleague helpfully notes that bears have been known to be attracted to women at certain times of the month. "Bears can smell the menstruation."

"Well, that's just great," Brian Fantana, the news team's crack reporter, says to the station manager. "You hear that, Ed? Bears. Now you're putting the whole station in jeopardy."

Later in the film, when Burgundy is squiring Veronica Corningstone, his new female co-anchor, around San Diego, he drives her to the cliffs above town to show her the view. "Mmm. San Diego. Drink it in, it always goes down smooth. Discovered by the Germans in 1904. They named it 'San Diego,' which of course in German means 'a whale's vagina.'"

Corningstone responds, "No, there's no way that's correct."

This time, Burgundy comes clean. "I'm sorry, I was trying to impress you. I don't know what it means. I'll be honest, I don't think anyone knows what it means anymore. Scholars maintain that the translation was lost hundreds of years ago."

"Doesn't it mean 'Saint Diego'?" asks Corningstone.

"No. No," Burgundy confidently responds.

"No, that's—that's what it means. Really."

"Well. Agree to disagree," Burgundy replies in a rare moment of conciliation.

Why am I bringing all of this up?

Let me answer that question with a question: What's the difference between Chris Matthews and Ron Burgundy? Answer: One is a pompous, self-absorbed, often-in-error-but-never-in-doubt blowhard impervious to facts and logic. The other has a really bushy mustache.

Ron Burgundy believed that "San Diego" was German for a whale's lady parts; meanwhile, Matthews seems to believe that "Chicago" is English—or at least Republican English—for "den of panhandling negroes." By now you've probably heard about the exchange on MSNBC between *New York* magazine's John Heilemann and Matthews in which the two worked out the hidden code in Republican politics. "They keep saying

'Chicago,'" Matthews said. "That's another thing that sends that message—this guy's helping the poor people in the bad neighborhoods, screwing us in the 'burbs."

Heilemann nodded, adding, "There's a lot of black people in Chicago."

Indeed there are. Though it's worth noting that the Windy City is still more white than black. Its mayor, Rahm Emanuel, who just happens to have been Obama's chief of staff, isn't particularly dark-skinned. Oh, and Barack Obama, the incumbent president, launched and built his entire political career in Chicago, a city synonymous with cutthroat machine politics for more than a century. And it's where the Obama reelection headquarters are. Countless white reporters at the *New York Times*, NBC, NPR, the *Washington Post*, and elsewhere use the term "Chicago" as a shorthand for the Obama campaign. But when Republicans say "Chicago" (which few did at the Republican convention, by the way), there can be no doubt: It's a stand-in for the N-word.

Never mind that the charge that Obama is a big-city liberal who wants to redistribute more wealth from the haves to the have-nots is actually true. I could recycle all of Obama's quotes about fairness and spreading the wealth around. I could walk you through the food-stamp numbers under Obama and the increased progressivity he wants in the tax code. I could even present selections from *The Audacity of Hope*. But that's the problem. That would be racist, too. Because the key factor in determining whether something is racist is whether it is inconvenient to Barack Obama.

When MSNBC got an advance copy of Senate minority leader Mitch McConnell's convention speech, the network landed another scoop. "For four years," McConnell planned to say, "Barack Obama has been running from the nation's problems. He hasn't been working to earn reelection. He has been working to earn a spot on the PGA Tour." A fool might think this a not-exactly-veiled reference to the fact that Barack

Obama plays a lot of golf, more than 100 rounds since he was elected. But MSNBC's Lawrence O'Donnell is no fool.

Asked what he made of the line, O'Donnell confidently replied, "Well, we know exactly what he's trying to do there. He's trying to align . . . the lifestyle of Tiger Woods with Barack Obama."

Martin Bashir asked O'Donnell whether he really believed that. Couldn't McConnell just mean what he said?

O'Donnell went into full eye-roll mode. "Martin, there are many, many, many rhetorical choices you can make at any point in any speech to make whatever point you want to make." According to O'Donnell, McConnell's speechwriters chose the golf reference because "these people reach for every single possible racial double entendre they can find in every one of these speeches."

Bashir, who for a moment gave the impression of neural activity, was convinced. "Wow," he exclaimed. "Things are getting lower and lower by the day."

When Robert Welch of the John Birch Society insisted that Dwight Eisenhower was a Communist, Russell Kirk famously retorted, "He's not a Communist, he's a golfer." Thank goodness no one knew back then that Kirk was calling Ike a sexually promiscuous half-black man.

What O'Donnell says about Republican speechwriters strikes me as a near-perfect example of projection. It's not that McConnell's speechwriters are reaching for "every racial double entendre they can." But O'Donnell, Matthews, et al. are. It's a hallmark of the paranoid style. The Birchers, for instance, acted as though all it took to prove a Communist conspiracy was to mention one. Something analogous goes for the "dog whistlers" who hear coded messages in everything, even when the intended recipients don't. (Indeed, it seems lost on so many of the experts that the Romney campaign's whole strategy of trying to woo former Obama voters to their side is at odds with the racism thesis. After all, people who've already voted for a black guy probably aren't all that racist in the first place.)

Not everyone in the press is so Ron Burgundyesque. Tom Edsall, one of the more esteemed members of the fourth estate, a former *Washington Post* reporter and now a professor at the Columbia School of Journalism, penned a long analysis for the *New York Times* blowing the lid off Romney's race-baiting campaign. "The racial overtones of Romney's welfare ads are relatively explicit," he writes. The dictionary on my computer says "explicit" means "stated clearly and in detail, leaving no room for confusion or doubt." Oddly, if you watch Romney's welfare ads, there's no mention of race in any way. Edsall must have a different dictionary. He then writes that the racial messaging in Romney's Medicare ads is "a bit more subtle." In those ads, Romney charges—accurately—that Obama raided Medicare to pay for Obamacare.

Aha! But Medicare recipients, Edsall notes, are "overwhelmingly white." Which is true! The health-care entitlement for the elderly goes mostly to white people. You know why? Because the over-65 demographic is overwhelmingly white. And therefore what? Democrats have been demagoguing Medicare—"Mediscaring"—for nearly half a century. It's only when Republicans turn the tables on them that the press suddenly discovers that defending Medicare is really a sop to geriatric white nationalists. Or something.

A more subtle—and traditional—effort to racialize the GOP at convention time is to note "the sea of white faces" watching the speeches from the floor. And while it's true that the GOP delegates are awfully pale compared with Democratic convention-goers, it's difficult to find an example of a reporter's referring to the rigid racial-, ethnic-, and gender-quota system that goes a long way toward producing Democratic audiences that "look like America." And whenever the Republicans gave prominent speaker slots to minority or female Republicans, the reflex was to discount their participation as so much window-dressing (on the first night of the Republican convention, MSNBC cut away to its resident race-baiters whenever a non-white was speaking). Shouldn't those who claim to be concerned about the GOP's attitude toward minorities celebrate such outreach? Why is (alleged) tokenism among Republican speakers so contemptible but tokenism among Democratic attendees so unremarkable?

In one of the most memorable scenes in *Anchorman*, Brian Fantana explains that his cologne is so effective with the ladies that "60 percent of the time, it works every time." This seems to be the standard adhered to by another branch of the press corps: the fact-checkers. These self-appointed arbiters of all truth have become an invaluable resource for reporters and liberal columnists too weary to do their own research or make their own arguments. Instead, they simply cite a fact-checker's conclusion as if it were dispositive. It's a strange practice. If I were to write a column that said "Joe Shmoe says Barack Obama killed a man in Reno just to watch him die" and then proceeded to act as if that were all the proof required, it wouldn't pass muster with anyone. But if Joe Shmoe had deputized himself with a construction-paper badge that said "fact-checker," all of a sudden his opinion would be metaphysical truth.

Paul Ryan has been the most prominent victim of the fact-check schtick. A particularly odd form of madness overtook the so-called mainstream media the night Ryan gave his acceptance speech in Tampa. From the outside, it looked like the establishment political press was receiving Obama campaign tweets straight through their fillings: Ryan was a liar! "The verdict," reported the *Washington Post*, "rendered by a slew of media fact checkers, was immediate and unequivocal: In his first major speech before the American people, the Republican vice presidential nominee repeatedly left out key facts, ignored context and was blind to his own hypocrisy."

Liberal Media Bias

Surveys over the past 25 years have consistently found that journalists are much more liberal than the rest of America.

- *Journalists Vote for Liberals*: Between 1964 and 2004, Republicans won the White House seven times compared with four Democratic victories. But if only journalists' ballots were counted, the Democrats would have won every time.

- *Journalists Say They Are Liberal*: Surveys from 1978 to 2005 show that journalists are far more likely to say they are liberal than conservative, and are far more liberal than the public at large.

- *Journalists Reject Conservative Positions*: None of the surveys have found that news organizations are populated by independent thinkers who mix liberal and conservative positions. Most journalists offer reflexively liberal answers to practically every question a pollster can imagine.

- *The Public Recognizes the Bias*: Nearly nine out of ten Americans believe journalists sometimes or often let their personal views influence the way they report the news, and most say this bias helps liberals. Even a plurality of Democrats agree the press is liberal.

- *Denials of Liberal Bias*. Many journalists continue to deny the liberal bias that taints their profession.

- *Admissions of Liberal Bias*. A number of journalists have admitted that the majority of their brethren approach the news from a liberal angle.

Media Research Center, "The Liberal Media Exposed," 2007.

Really? The fact-checkers diagnosed Ryan with blindness to his own hypocrisy? That's a neat trick.

The only problem: Everything Ryan said was true. Nearly every charge of lying boiled down to Ryan's not raising counterarguments favorable to Obama—a standard not normally applied to politicians, and certainly never considered the litmus test for truth-telling. Notoriously, Ryan noted that in 2008 Obama suggested that an auto plant in Ryan's district that was scheduled for closure would stay open for 100 years if he was elected. The fact-checkers and Obama campaign surrogates immediately cried foul: The plant, they said, actually closed under Bush! But the AP ignored its own (accurate) reporting on the plant's closing in 2009 in order to make its "fact check" as damning as possible. The second problem: Ryan's point was not that Obama's prediction was factually wrong, but that Obama over-promised. That's what Obama does: Fish gotta swim, bird gotta fly, Obama needs to promise the moon. The fact-checkers opted to twist Ryan's point into something he wasn't saying, and then charged him with lying for saying it.

More recently, a *Washington Post* fact-checker waded into a debate over Barack Obama's stance on abortion. After a long and convoluted discussion, the fact-checker conceded, reluctantly, that yes, Obama did oppose legislation that would protect babies who survived abortions. Obama has denied this and accused anyone who says otherwise of lying. But rather than give Obama a poor score, the fact-checker punted: "The evidence suggests we could have awarded Four Pinocchios [their worst score] to the former Illinois Senator for his comments . . . but that interview is several years old now, and it's not the focus of this particular column."

How convenient! The *Post* can't even identify Obama by name as the politician deserving of the dreaded four scarlet

"P"s. He's merely the former Illinois senator who deserves to be called a liar about his support for infanticide—but we're too sleepy to bother.

What makes media bias so infuriating is not its existence but the stubborn refusal of the guilty parties to admit it. It's all part of the larger con of American liberalism, which sees itself as immune to ideology, on the side of facts and logic and all things "pragmatic." The mainstream press simply won't admit the obvious, reality-based truth: They are a de facto arm of American liberalism. To paraphrase Ron Burgundy, it's not "the media," it's the liberal media—and that is a scientific fact.

| *"The news media tend to give conserva-tives a very big megaphone."*

There Is a Conservative Media Bias

John Merline

John Merline is a senior writer at Investor's Business Daily. *In the following viewpoint, he investigates claims of a conservative media bias, finding that conservative political candidates and commentators get significantly more media coverage than liberal ones. He compares coverage of comparable liberals and conserva-tives in 2010: Sarah Palin and Joe Biden, Christine O'Donnell and Alvin Greene, and television commentators Glenn Beck and Keith Olbermann. In every case, he argues, the conservative has received much more media attention than the liberal. Merline contends that the mainstream media focuses on conservatives and gives them a forum from which to disseminate their policies and ideology. If used effectively, he says, this can be a key politi-cal advantage.*

As you read, consider the following questions:

1. According to a Pew Research Center survey, cited by the author, what political party held the top three spots of the top ten most-covered candidates in the 2010 midterm elections?

2. What ratio of media coverage did Sarah Palin have to Joe Biden's in 2010, according to Merline's investigation?

3. In what place was Keith Olbermann's show rated on MSNBC in 2010, as reported by the author?

Almost exactly a year ago [in December 2009], liberal talk show host Keith Olbermann went on a rant about the right-wing bias in the media. "There is no liberal media," he said. "The media which is, after all, owned by corporations, naturally leans to the right. Corporations, by definition, lean to the right, towards the status quo."

Conservatives scoffed at the notion. But maybe Olbermann has a point.

After all, when it comes to conservatives, reporters can't seem to get enough of them.

Indeed, a Pew Research Center survey found that of the top 10 most-covered candidates in the midterm [2010] elections, conservatives held the top three spots.

Here's more evidence. I asked AOL's Relegence team, which tracks more than 30,000 news sites on the Web, to compare coverage of comparable liberals and conservatives over the past 12 months.

The results are stark. Conservatives were featured in vastly more stories.

Examples of Conservative Media Bias

Here are three illustrative examples.

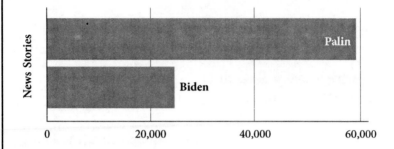

Media Coverage: Sarah Palin vs. Joe Biden

Total number of 2008 news stories that prominently featured the Republican (Palin) or Democratic (Biden) nominee for vice-president

TAKEN FROM: John Merline, "Conservative Media Bias Exposed?," *AOL News*, December 23, 2010. www.aolnews.com.

Palin vs. Biden

On the conservative side is Sarah Palin, the gaffe-prone politician who occasionally lapses into blue language and lost her bid for vice president in the 2008 election. On the other side is Joe Biden, the winning 2008 vice presidential candidate, who's also prone to misspeak and use blue language.

While Palin is a publicity hound, Biden actually has a hold on the reins of power. Presumably, what he thinks and does matters in the real world, unlike Palin.

So who got more coverage? There's no contest. There were, according to Relegence, almost 62,000 stories in which Palin figured prominently—almost *three times* the number that featured Biden. There wasn't a single month in 2010 where Biden got more coverage than Palin. . . .

O'Donnell vs. Greene

Conservative Christine O'Donnell was an unqualified, kooky candidate who took everyone by surprise when she beat a far better known, established candidate for the Republican Senate nomination in Delaware. Liberal Alvin Greene was a completely unqualified, kooky candidate who also shocked everyone by getting the Democratic nomination for Senate over four-term South Carolina state lawmaker Vic Rawl. Both went on to decisively lose their elections.

Now it's true that O'Donnell was a character, but so too was Greene, who had a felony charge on his record and had never campaigned for the nomination. Plus there was concern that the electronic voting systems might have failed in South Carolina, causing Greene's win. But while the media went gaga over O'Donnell, by comparison they ignored Greene. . . .

Beck vs. Olbermann

As everyone with a pulse knows, Glenn Beck is the sometimes controversial host of the No. 4 rated show on Fox News. And Olbermann is the sometimes controversial host of the No. 1 show on MSNBC.

On which gum-flapper did the press shower more coverage? You guessed it. Beck crushed Olbermann. Month after month, Beck racked up hundreds, if not thousands, of stories. In contrast, Olbermann typically only got a few dozen stories a month in which he was featured prominently—except for the month when he was temporarily suspended. . . .

This is, admittedly, a small sample, and there are no doubt some counterexamples. Plus, the data don't capture tone or message of this coverage. But my guess is that if you looked at other newsmakers on the right you'd find a similar pattern.

Are these conservatives really that much more newsworthy than their liberal counterparts?

That seems highly unlikely.

So what is the reason? Is it a right-wing tilt, along the lines Olbermann complained about? Or is it that liberal reporters just find conservatives and their ideas more unfamiliar, odd or just plain worrisome, making their utterances appear more worthy of coverage?

I'll leave it to the media watchdogs on both sides to battle over what bias is at work here.

But whatever the motivation, one this is clear: The news media tend to give conservatives a very big megaphone.

> *"When all is said and done, left-leaning reporting is balanced by reporting more favorable to conservatives."*

There Is No Significant Media Bias

Paul Farhi

Paul Farhi is a reporter for the Washington Post *and senior contributing writer for the* American Journalism Review. *In the following viewpoint, he contends that the pervasive belief that the mainstream media is biased is more perception than reality. Farhi contends that although researchers investigating the issue have found bias in reporting, it has not uncovered any persuasive evidence that one side is consistently favored over the other. In fact, he says, news reporting favors the center because that is where the advertising money is. He traces the perception of media bias to the emergence of partisan cable and Internet news sources, the prevalence of media watchdog groups, the misperception that commentary is news coverage, and other factors.*

As you read, consider the following questions:

1. According to a 2011 Pew Research Center study cited by Farhi, what percentage of people say that the media "tend to favor one side"?

2. What percentage of the respondents in the Pew study think of cable news when they hear the phrase "news organization," as reported by the author?

3. What percentage of the respondents in the Pew study, according to Fahi, say that news organizations are "often inaccurate"?

Charges of media bias have been flying like a bloody banner on the campaign trail. Newt Gingrich excoriated the "elite media" in a richly applauded moment during one of the Republican debates. Rick Santorum chewed out a *New York Times* reporter. Mitt Romney said this month [April 2012] that he faces "an uphill battle" against the press in the general election.

Meanwhile, just about every new poll of public sentiment shows that confidence in the news media has hit a new low. Seventy-seven percent of those surveyed by the Pew Research Center in the fall [of 2011] said the media "tend to favor one side" compared with 53 percent who said so in 1985.

But have the media really become more biased? Or is this a case of perception trumping reality?

In fact, there's little to suggest that over the past few decades news reporting has become more favorable to one party. That's not to say researchers haven't found bias in reporting. They have, but they don't agree that one side is consistently favored or that this favoritism has been growing like a pernicious weed.

Investigating Media Bias

On the conservative side, the strongest case might have been made by Tim Groseclose, a political science and economics professor at the University of California at Los Angeles. Groseclose used a three-pronged test to quantify the "slant quotient" of news stories reported by dozens of media sources. He compared these ratings with a statistical analysis of the voting records of various national politicians. In his 2011 book *Left Turn: How Liberal Bias Distorts the American Mind*, Groseclose concluded that most media organizations aligned with the views of liberal politicians. (Groseclose determined that *The Washington Post*'s "slant quotient" was less liberal than news coverage in the *New York Times* and *Wall Street Journal*.)

Even with conservative-leaning sources such as the *Drudge Report* and the *Washington Times* factored in, "the aggregate slant is leftward," said Groseclose, who describes himself as a conservative.

But that's not the end of the story. A "meta-analysis" of bias studies—that is, a study of studies—shows something different: When all is said and done, left-leaning reporting is balanced by reporting more favorable to conservatives. "The net effect is zero," said David D'Alessio, a communications sciences professor at the University of Connecticut at Stamford.

D'Alessio drew his conclusion from reviewing 99 studies of campaign news coverage undertaken over six decades for his newly published work, *Media Bias in Presidential Election Coverage 1948–2008: Evaluation via Formal Measurement*. The research, he says, shows that news reporting tends to point toward the middle, "because that's where the people are, and that's where the [advertising] money is. . . . There's nuance there, but when you add it all and subtract it down, you end up with nothing."

So why the rise in the public's perception of media bias? A few possibilities . . . .

The Media Landscape Has Changed

There's more media and more overtly partisan media outlets, too. The Internet has given rise to champions of the left—

Huffington Post, Daily Kos, etc.—as well as more conservative organizations such as *Drudge* and *Free Republic*. This means your chance of running into "news" that seems biased has increased exponentially, elevating the impression that "bias" is pervasive throughout all parts of the media.

"There's a kind of self-fulfilling perception to it," said Robert Lichter, a pioneering media-bias researcher who heads the *Center for Media and Public Affairs* at George Mason University. "Once people see something they don't like, they notice things that reinforce the belief that there's bias" in the media as a whole.

More Bias-Hunting Watchdog Groups

Long ago, a few watchdog groups, such as the conservative AIM (Accuracy in Media) and its more liberal counterpart FAIR (Fairness and Accuracy in Reporting), kept an eye on reporters' work. Nowadays, not just politicians criticize the media for their alleged bias; an entire cottage industry exists to highlight the media's alleged failings. This includes ideological outfits such as Media Matters for America and the Media Research Center; the satirical "Daily Show" and "Colbert Report"; and blogs by the hundreds.

All that scrutiny of the press may suggest an inescapable conclusion: There's something wrong with the news media. All the time.

Journalists have gotten that message, too. "Reporters have heard the criticism from the right so often that they lean over backwards to be fair to them," said Eric Alterman, a journalist, college professor and the author of the best-selling *What Liberal Media? The Truth About Bias and the News*.

News Reporting vs. Commentary

Few people make a distinction between news reporting— which attempts to play it straight—and opinion-mongering, which is designed to provoke and persuade. Tellingly, when

asked what they think of when they hear the phrase "news organization," the majority of respondents (63 percent) in Pew's news-bias survey cited "cable news," and specifically Fox News and CNN. But while cable news networks do some straightforward reporting, their most popular programs, by far, are those in which opinionated hosts ask opinionated guests to sling opinions about the day's news.

"A big part of the conversation on cable is [people] telling you how the rest of the media is getting the story wrong," said Mark Jurkowitz, a former press critic and newspaper ombudsman who is now associate director of the Project for Excellence in Journalism, a Washington-based research group affiliated with Pew. That, he noted, is likely to sow more doubt about the media's integrity or accuracy.

Of course, reporters have helped blur the very lines they want the public to respect, Lichter said, by writing up news stories and then appearing on TV or going on social media to tell people what to think about their stories.

"The modern way [for journalists] is to be edgy and opinionated and to call attention to yourself," Lichter said.

Expanded Coverage of News

Thanks to technology, people have more access to more sources of news than before. Which means they can check several accounts of the same event. This can create its own kind of suspicion; savvy readers often ask reporters why they ignored or played down facts that another reporter emphasized.

Pew's research suggests that people think the other guy's media are spreading lies while one's own are, relatively, a paragon of truth.

A clear majority (66 percent) say news organizations in general are "often inaccurate." But the figure drops precipitously (to 30 percent) when people are asked the same question about the news organization "you use most." Jurkowitz said this is the analogue of how people feel about Congress—most give low marks to lawmakers in general, but they vote to reelect their incumbent representative more than 90 percent of the time.

"If you watch the Channel 2 newscast night after night, you trust the people on the air," he said. "The mere fact that you're a habituated user makes you think better of them."

Despite the low esteem the public seems to hold for "the news media," the good news may be that it's all relative. Pew found last year that people said they trusted information from the news media more than any other source, including state governments, the [Barack] Obama administration, federal government agencies, corporations and Congress.

The lowest degree of trust? By far, people named "candidates running for office."

> *"The narrative of the [2012 presiden-*
> *tial] campaign . . . has worked heavily*
> *in Obama's favor . . . [and] the domi-*
> *nant narrative writers of the campaign*
> *are the national media."*

The Biased Media Is Trying to Influence Political Elections

L. Brent Bozell III

L. Brent Bozell III is a conservative writer, syndicated columnist, and founder of the Media Research Center. In the following viewpoint, he maintains that the liberal media bias during the 2012 presidential campaign was so profound that it influenced the electorate toward Barack Obama. Bozell argues that the news media successfully created a dominant narrative that the Republican challenger, Mitt Romney, was an unacceptable choice and gave President Obama a massive promotional advantage in the campaign. It was clear, Bozell states, that the media was hounding Mitt Romney while letting President Obama off the hook on several troubling matters. He contends that the media should be ashamed of themselves for influencing the election in such a blatant manner and that viewers should turn away from traditional news sources who exhibit such a pronounced bias.

As you read, consider the following questions:

1. According to a July 2012 *Washington Post* poll cited by Bozell, what percentage of Americans approved of President Obama's handling of the economy?

2. What percentage of the network news stories about Mitt Romney's trip to Europe and Israel in 2012 were negative, according to the author?

3. What American president did CBS interviewer Steve Kroft compare Barack Obama to in 2007, according to Bozell?

On August 5 [2012], Chris Cillizza at *The Washington Post* announced he was playing with a "somewhat controversial idea" that Mitt Romney should be the favorite to win the presidential election. Debatable, maybe. But controversial? Well, yes. It violates the pro-Obama mandate of our national press corps.

The usual political measures look terrible for Obama, he noted. "The unemployment rate has been over 8 percent for 42 straight months, a streak unparalleled in American history." Obama must win despite the crippled economy—the most important issue for the voters.

The numbers are political red alerts. The *Post*'s polling in July [2012] showed 44 percent approved of how Obama was dealing with the economy, while 54 percent disapproved, and 41 strongly disapproved of the job he is doing on the economy, while only 21 percent strongly approved. Six in ten said the economy was getting worse, not better, in a Gallup poll.

And now the unthinkable: His campaign is being outmuscled financially. Obama's team has spent more than $400 million already on his re-election effort, *The New York Times* estimates, and Team Obama is deeply worried he will be outspent by Mitt Romney and GOP-favoring super PACs [political action committees] in the fall.

Who Creates the Narrative?

So where can Obama find optimism? Cillizza cited the "narrative." "From the debate over when Romney totally cut ties to Bain Capital, to the (ongoing) debate over whether he should release more of his tax returns, to the negative press surrounding Romney's trip to Britain, Israel and Poland last week [in August 2012], the narrative of the campaign over the past month has worked heavily in Obama's favor."

Curiously, Cillizza omits the fact that the dominant narrative writers of the campaign are the national media, our "news" purveyors, working overtime on Obama's behalf. Reporters pin down the candidate, slap his face, and steal his lunch money, and then go on camera and say it's sad the candidate had another bad day with his narrative. When Barack Obama was hailed by crowds in Berlin in 2008, the media were thrilled. When Romney traveled to Europe and Israel in 2012, 86 percent of the network news stories were negative, dwelling on supposed gaffes, "diplomatic dust-ups" and foreign "missteps."

In nearly every interview, reporters are pressing Romney about his tax returns, rolling out the red carpet for anyone who will demand he release them immediately. Can you imagine reporters in 2008 asking Obama repeatedly for his college grades, or about his cocaine use, or Reverend [Jeremiah] Wright, in interview after interview?

Obama granted five interviews to *60 Minutes* before that election, and was *never* asked about his record in Illinois, or any of his scandalous associations, from Reverend Wright to [activist/radio host] Bill Ayers to [Chicago businessman convicted of fraud] Tony Rezko (now in prison), who helped him buy his house. Instead, [*60 Minutes* reporter] Steve Kroft asked in his first interview "Do you think the country is ready for a black president?" Kroft was still curious in his fifth interview, as they sat down in apparently racism-wracked Nevada: "I know, for a fact, that there are a lot of people out there, there

The Reverend Jeremiah Wright

Jeremiah A. Wright Jr. is one of the most widely acclaimed Christian ministers in the United States. Combining social concern, spiritual growth, and political activism, Wright preaches in a traditional African-American style, bringing a message of hope, redemption, and renewal. In 1972 he became pastor of a small United Church of Christ (UCC) congregation in inner-city Chicago. During his more than 35 years in the pulpit, his congregation grew to 10,000 members and became the largest UCC congregation in the United States. While Wright has long been one of the nation's most visible black clergymen, it was his association with the 2008 presidential campaign of Barack Obama and his fiery rhetoric during the hard-fought Democratic primary battle—including a sermon perceived by many as anti-American—that ultimately brought him national attention.

Gale Biography in Context,
"Jeremiah A. Wright Jr.," 2013.

are a lot of people right here in Elko, who won't vote for you because you're black. I mean, there's not much you can do. But how do you deal with it?"

Media Bias and Its Effect

Ultimately Barack Obama will never be outspent—if you were to calculate the price of the promotional air time provided by the pro-Obama media, and in this cycle, their relentless Romney-bashing. While the networks manufacture gaffes overseas with Romney, real Obama gaffes—"If you've got a business, you didn't build that"—are called Republican smears, quotes out of "context."

In an online analysis, ABC [network] claimed Republicans were basically lying: "Republicans have seized on the line 'you didn't build that' to falsely claim that Obama was speaking directly to business owners about their businesses." On CBS, morning anchor Charlie Rose complained about Obama being taken out of context, and the network's political analyst, John Dickerson, agreed that Obama needed to be defended: "Exactly, and what the President was saying, is it takes a village, essentially."

When Obama said "Look, if you've been successful, you didn't get there on your own," he knew whereof he spoke. Everything he's gained in politics has been granted to him by an adoring news media. Look no further than Steve Kroft beginning his first Obama interview in 2007 by seriously comparing Obama with Abraham Lincoln.

It's no surprise that many voters have a serious feeling of buyer's remorse. But our shameless media have no remorse at all for foisting this man on the country, and no capacity for embarrassment that they put him on Mount Rushmore without an accomplishment to his name. It's too bad America can't vote to send the media packing. But they can, and should turn off the nightly narratives lamely called a "newscast."

> *"Liberal bias in the media is . . . a lot of nonsense, cooked up by conservatives to be used as a kind of stick with which to beat journalists in the hope of getting better coverage."*

Charges of Media Bias Are an Attempt to Influence Media Coverage

Eric Alterman

Eric Alterman is an author, a columnist for the Nation *magazine, a senior fellow at the Center for American Progress, and a distinguished professor of English and journalism at Brooklyn College in New York City. In the following viewpoint, he charges that recent complaints of liberal media bias by conservative politicians and media were made to influence media coverage of the 2012 presidential election. Alterman argues that claims of liberal media bias are rarely backed up by specific examples or evidence of partisanship and have been cooked up by conservatives to get more favorable media coverage for their candidates. Several right-wing commentators have actually admitted it over the years, he contends.*

As you read, consider the following questions:

1. According to Nate Silver, cited by Alterman, what was the bias on average across 240 US Senate races since 1990?

2. What percentage of climate scientists embrace the scientific consensus on global warming, according to the author?

3. What does Alterman report happened when the *Washington Post* intended to hire a right-wing blogger?

Last Sunday [September 29, 2012], on the very same morning when he complained on *Meet the Press* that the mainstream media were, in his view, treating Republican presidential candidate Mitt Romney more harshly than President Barack Obama (of course without presenting any evidence), Gov. Chris Christie (R-NJ) admitted on ABC's *This Week*, "I'm not going to sit here and complain about coverage of the campaign because, as a candidate, if you do that, you're losing."

Ditto Rep. Paul Ryan (R-WI), the former Massachusetts governor's vice presidential running mate. Appearing (apparently without irony) on *Fox News Sunday*, the show that brought Rep. Ryan a birthday cake and whose moderator, Chris Wallace, bragged that "we kind of discovered" him, Rep. Ryan insisted that "it kind of goes without saying that there's a media bias," adding, "We've—look, I'm a conservative person, I'm used to media bias. We expected media bias going into this." But like Gov. Christie, Rep. Ryan did not have any specifics in mind when asked to present an example. And later, he sort of took it back—or at least his spokesman did. In an email to *Politico*, the spokesman insisted that Rep. Ryan "did not blame the media. He was asked a question about media bias and answered it. And his answer made clear it's not something he worries about."

A Provocative Letter

One thing that many conservatives profess to worry about of late is polling. In a letter addressed to what they called the "Biased News Media," conservative leaders Brent Bozell, Gary Bauer, Ed Meese, Tony Perkins, Rush Limbaugh, and Richard Viguerie signed a letter authored by Bozell's right-wing Media Research Center, "holding the liberal media accountable for shamelessly advancing a left-wing agenda." The signatories argued: "This election year, so much of the broadcast networks, their cable counterparts and the major establishment print media are out of control with a deliberate and unmistakable leftist agenda." Again, not much in the way of evidence was presented.

Polling

The issue of alleged bias that most excites conservatives this year [2012] is polling. The purpose of this year's polls, according to Rush Limbaugh, is not to take the pulse of any given election contents. Rather, "they are designed to do exactly what [Rush has] warned you to be vigilant about, and that is to depress you and suppress your vote. These two polls today are designed to convince everybody this election is over." Again, zero evidence from Rushbo. And according to [polling reporting website] FiveThirtyEight's Nate Silver, that would be awfully surprising. As he explains, "The polls have no such history of partisan bias, at least not on a consistent basis."

Polling is a decidedly inexact science and is never perfectly accurate, even allowing for changes in peoples' minds over time. Silver explains:

> There have been years, like 1980 and 1994, when the polls did underestimate the standing of Republicans. But there have been others, like 2000 and 2006, when they underestimated the standing of Democrats.... but as in the case of the presidential polls, the years in which the Senate polls missed in either direction have tended to cancel one another

out. On average across 240 Senate races since 1990, the polls have had a Republican bias of just 0.4 percentage points, a trivial number that is of little meaning statistically.

Add up all of the above and you have a great many accusations—some withdrawn, some not—but not a whole heck of a lot of data to support a single one of them. It may be because they are absolutely correct but that liberal bias in the media is so sneaky it disappears before you can catch it, quantify it, or even identify a compelling example of its persistence. Then again, it may be because the entire notion is a lot of nonsense, cooked up by conservatives to be used as a kind of stick with which to beat journalists in the hope of getting better coverage.

Working the Refs

Think I'm making this up? Just ask Rich Bond, who, as the then-chair of the Republican Party, complained during the 1992 election, "I think we know who the media want to win this election—and I don't think it's George [H.W.] Bush." That was Bond on a bad day. On one of his truth-telling days, however, the very same Mr. Bond observed of the very same election, however, "There is some strategy to it [bashing the 'liberal' media]. . . . if you watch any great coach, what they try to do is 'work the refs.' Maybe the ref will cut you a little slack on the next one."

This latter sentiment is not really so rare among conservatives, at least the ones who understand that they are playing a game. Far-right pundit and sometime presidential candidate Pat Buchanan admitted, "I've gotten balanced coverage, and broad coverage—all we could have asked. For heaven sakes, we kid about the 'liberal media,' but every Republican on earth does that."

And conservative standard-bearer William Kristol told *The New Yorker*, upon launching *The Weekly Standard* back in 1995, that "the liberal media were never that powerful, and

Rush Limbaugh

Limbaugh began a lifelong love affair with radio broadcasting in his hometown of Cape Girardeau, Missouri, where, as a teenager, he worked for the local radio station. That love affair survived Limbaugh's rocky career as an itinerant broadcast journalist in various cities until he developed his unique talk-show format in Sacramento beginning in 1984. In 1988 he moved his show to New York City and began broadcasting to a nationwide audience. He now touts himself as "the number-one talk-show host in America"—and his claim is no empty boast, for *The Rush Limbaugh Show* has become a broadcasting phenomenon. Each afternoon, "Rush" attracts over a million-and-a-half fans who tune in to over 500 stations around the country to hear his blustery, irreverent views on political topics. . . .

Limbaugh has achieved success with an unlikely agenda—conservative politics. The show's substance is a provocative defense of Limbaugh's version of the traditional, mainstream American values he says he inherited from his father. Limbaugh continually skewers his pet targets—primarily liberal special-interest groups, including, in his words, environmental "wackos," feminists, the "arts and croissant people," and "pencil-neck geeks." His constant theme is the absurdities to which he believes "commie-liberals" run in their zeal over one social cause or another. While Limbaugh touts a conservative political agenda, another aspect of his popularity is his unflagging showmanship. Typical is a continuing skit aimed at animal rights activists: as part of an "animal rights update," he plays an Andy Williams recording of the song "Born Free" with the sounds of gunshots and animals screaming in the background.

Gale Biography in Context, *"Rush Limbaugh,"* 2013.

the whole thing was often used as an excuse by conservatives for conservative failures." Even so, in a 2001 subscriber pitch for the magazine, Kristol complained, "The trouble with politics and political coverage today is that there's too much liberal bias. . . . there's too much tilt toward the left-wing agenda. Too much apology for liberal policy failures. Too much pandering to liberal candidates and causes."

A "Great Little Racket"

This constant confusion—you might even call it "flip-flopping"—was finally explained in 2003 by *The Weekly Standard* "senior writer" and Kristol protégé Matt Labash, who told the website JournalismJobs.com:

> While all these hand-wringing Freedom Forum types talk about objectivity, the conservative media likes to rap the liberal media on the knuckles for not being objective. We've created this cottage industry in which it pays to be unobjective. It pays to be subjective as much as possible. It's a great way to have your cake and eat it too. Criticize other people for not being objective. Be as subjective as you want. It's a great little racket. I'm glad we found it, actually.

It sure is. And after all this time, it still works. Take, for instance, last Sunday's [early October 2012] *Washington Post* ombudsman's column "Will *The Post* be about news or opinion?" by Patrick Pexton. In it, Pexton rehearses the usual complaints from Republicans about alleged liberal bias in the *Post*'s coverage both in polls of conservatives and his own email box. He finds this upswing in conservative complaints significant because, when combined with recent polling data that reflect a similar degree of discontent, these feelings must, Pexton opines, reflect a reality of unfair coverage. Again, Mr. Pexton does not deal in such mundane details as evidence, but observes that "with the exception of Dan Balz and Chris Cillizza, who cover politics in a nonpartisan way, the news columnists almost to a person write from left of center."

Actually, this is not true. They may or may not hold left-of-center views, but most of them are data driven. The biggest problem conservatives have today is not with media but reality.

What Is Liberal Bias?

Is it "liberal" to refuse to deny the scientific consensus on global warming embraced by 97 percent of climate scientists? Is it liberal to note, along with almost all economists, including those who have served in Republican administrations, that tax cuts for the wealthy fail to improve tax revenues and succeed only in increasing inequality? Is it liberal to report the truth about the timing of factory closings in Wisconsin when a conservative candidate muffs it on purpose? What's more, Pexton has a strange idea of left of center, since it includes Dana Milbank, who thought it appropriate, on the *Post* website, to joke that Secretary of State Hillary Clinton was a "mad bitch."

Ironically, nowhere is the conservative flight from reality better illustrated than in the *Post*'s hapless attempts to hire a right-wing blogger. In doing so, they have easily found plagiarists, nonconservatives, and abusive, violence-inciting, race-baiting attack dogs. What they have yet to find is a qualified journalist.

Pexton concludes with a homily: "*The Post* should first be about news without slant. If *The Post* wants to wrap its news in commentary, fine, but shouldn't some of those voices then be conservative?"

Congratulations Mr. Bond. That ref-working strategy of yours is still going strong—after only 20 years.

| "A partisan press may be driving an increase in political involvement."

A Partisan Media May Inspire Participation and Interest in Political Issues

Paul Starr

Paul Starr is an author and professor of sociology and public affairs at Princeton University. In the following viewpoint, he traces the role of partisan media throughout US history. Starr examines the emergence of partisan media in the early years of the American republic, its fall by the start of the twentieth century as more-independent and objective media outlets prevailed, and then its reemergence in the late twentieth century. The resurgence of powerful partisan media outlets reflects the country's deepening political divisions, but does not have to be viewed as a completely negative trend, he argues, noting that it may spur political participation and passion for civic involvement. He adds, however, that it is important that journalists maintain professional standards in a world of partisan media.

As you read, consider the following questions:

1. According to Starr, what country had the highest per-capita newspaper circulation in the world by 1835?

Paul Starr, "Governing in the Age of Fox News," *Atlantic*, January–February 2011. Copyright © 2011 by the Atlantic. All rights reserved. Reproduced by permission.

2. What US president brought reporters into the White House on a regular basis, as reported by the author?

3. How many Americans watched President Obama's health care speech to Congress on September 9, 2009, according to Starr?

The fight between the Obama White House and Fox News may look like a replay of previous presidential conflicts with the media. After all, antagonism between presidents and elements of the press is a fine American tradition. But the Fox News phenomenon is different, and its development reflects a deeper change in the public itself that presents a new challenge for presidential leadership.

A Partisan Media

What was once an expansive mass public has lost some of its old breadth and, at its core, become more intense and combative. A growing percentage of people, especially among the young, no longer regularly follow the news in any medium, while those who remain the most attentive and engaged tend to be sharply polarized along ideological lines. On both ends of the political spectrum, people interested in politics increasingly view national leadership through the prism of the partisan media that dominate cable news, talk radio, and the blogosphere.

The Old Media

Before cable and the Internet, the way for a president to reach the national public was through national media that sought to appeal to audiences spanning the partisan divide. The major newspapers, wire services, and broadcast networks controlled the flow of news from Washington and the president's access to the channels of persuasion, yet they operated more or less according to the standards of professional journalism, and the White House could exercise plenty of leverage in its media relations by selectively leaking news and granting exclusive interviews. So despite sometimes antagonistic relations with the press, presidents were able to use it to reach a broad and relatively coherent national public.

But now that the old behemoths of the news are in decline, the unified public they assembled is fading, too. Neither the broadcast networks nor the newspapers have the reach they once did, raising concerns about whether the press will be able to serve its classic function as a watchdog over government. That problem also has a flip side. Precisely because the press is often critical of political leaders, it provides them legitimacy when it validates the grounds for their decisions. A press that is widely trusted by the public for its independence and integrity is also a resource for building consensus. Thus when the public sorts itself according to hostile, ideologically separate media—when the world of [trusted CBS News anchorman from 1962 to 1981] Walter Cronkite gives way to the world of [controversial conservative radio host and commentator] Glenn Beck and [controversial liberal MSNBC news commentator] Keith Olbermann—political leadership loses a consensus-building partner. This is the problem that faces Barack Obama. It is not, however, an unprecedented one.

The History of the US Media

To most Americans, at least until recently, it had long seemed a settled matter that the media should have no relationship with political parties—but that has not been the norm throughout American history, much less in other countries. In many democracies, newspapers and other media have developed in parallel with political parties (sometimes directly financed and controlled by them), while elsewhere the media have been independent, with no partisan connection. The prevailing model for how American presidents interact with the media has gone through three historical stages. As a young republic (and to a large extent even after the Civil War), the nation had partisan newspapers; the second stage, stretching across the 20th century, was characterized by powerful, independent media outlets that kept their distance from the parties; and in the third stage, we now have a hybrid system that combines elements of the first two.

The founding period in American history created a new and richly supportive environment for the press. Britain and other European states, seeing popular newspapers as a political threat, had limited what they could say and imposed heavy taxes to raise their costs and reduce their circulation. America's Founders, in contrast, believed that the circulation of news and political debate could help preserve their fragile republic. So besides guaranteeing the press its freedom, they excluded it from taxation and subsidized its development by setting cheap postal rates for mailing newspapers to subscribers. The government thereby underwrote the costs of a national news network without regulating its content. Public officials also subsidized specific newspapers they favored, by awarding generous contracts for government printing and paying fees for official notices. Together with subscription and advertising income, the postal and printing subsidies provided the financial basis for a development of the press so rapid that by 1835, the United States, even though it was still almost entirely rural, probably had the highest per capita newspaper circulation in the world.

Government Subsidy of the Media

Under many regimes, government subsidies have made the press politically subservient. But in the United States, the postal subsidies benefited all newspapers without limitation based on viewpoint—and newspapers did clearly express their ideological stances. And because of the separation of powers and the federal system, printing subsidies from different branches and levels of government went to newspapers from different parties. In fact, rather than solidifying incumbent power, the early environment of the press paved the way for two insurgent presidential candidates, Thomas Jefferson in 1800 and Andrew Jackson in 1828.

The Power of the Press

Jefferson's Democratic-Republicans were the first party to exploit the press environment established by the Founders, and they did so despite adversity. In 1798, during an undeclared war with France, President John Adams's Federalists enacted the infamous Sedition Act, making it a crime to publish "false, scandalous and malicious writing" about the president (though not about the vice president, who at the time was none other than Jefferson himself, the leader of the opposition). The Adams administration used the act to prosecute leading Jeffersonian editors and close down their papers—but the Jeffersonians more than offset those losses by establishing dozens of new papers in the run-up to the election of 1800. In the process, they demonstrated that the press could serve as a lever for overturning power in the United States.

Political parties at this time were only loose coalitions of leaders; they had no ongoing organization except their newspapers, and in practice, the parties and their newspapers were almost indistinguishable. Local editors were key party organizers, and local party leaders often met in the newspaper office. According to some historians, this partisan press belonged to the "dark ages" of American journalism. But it played a central role in mobilizing political participation and creating a vibrant democracy. And at no time was that more the case than in 1828, when Jackson's supporters built a network of Democratic papers across the country, and voting turnout increased sharply.

A Shift in the Media Landscape

Once in office, Jackson established the practice (which lasted until 1860) of having a quasi-official paper that spoke directly for the president and received federal patronage. Still, the press continued to be highly competitive, and the presidential newspaper did not become a stable monopoly. In the 32 years following Jackson's election, 11 different papers in Washington served as presidential organs, and by the 1860s they were so outstripped in circulation by advertising-supported metropolitan dailies that a separate paper representing the president had become obsolete. Beginning with Lincoln, presidents communicated with the public through commercially financed newspapers, though many of these continued to have strong partisan identities.

The rise of the mass press inaugurated a long, second era in presidential communication, spanning most of the 20th century, when national leaders had to adapt to new realities, including the growing role of reporters as independent interpreters of the news and the development of media with national reach. In the late 19th century, presidents literally kept journalists at a distance (reporters had to wait outside the White House gates for news from officials coming and going). Presidents also did not represent themselves, nor were they seen, as the central actors in the nation's politics. Only at the turn of the century, as "congressional government" gave way to a stronger executive, did presidents begin to cultivate the press and make themselves more visible by seizing the opportunities for public persuasion and influence that mass communications provided.

The Impact of the Roosevelts

If Jefferson and Jackson were the two breakthrough presidents in the era of the partisan press, the two Roosevelts were their counterparts as presidential innovators in the mass media of the 20th century. Although the shift began under his predecessor, William McKinley, Theodore Roosevelt brought reporters into the White House on a more regular basis, providing them for the first time with a press room. He also projected his influence more widely, giving more speeches than earlier presidents had and making the most of his office as a "bully pulpit." With his charm and energy, Roosevelt infused the presidency with qualities that have served as a model for leadership through the media ever since.

Natural gifts were also critical to Franklin Roosevelt's [FDR's] success. The first Roosevelt, a Republican, had had the advantage of dealing with a press that was predominantly Republican in its sympathies. FDR, however, as a Democrat, was convinced that he needed to circumvent hostile Republican newspaper publishers to reach the public directly. Radio gave him that power. Unlike [his predecessor,] Herbert Hoover, Roosevelt spoke in a conversational style in his "fireside chats," creating the sense among his listeners that he was talking directly to them in their living rooms.

Television

The advent of television highlighted the personality and performative abilities of the president even more than had radio. What the fireside chat was for FDR, the televised news conference was for John F. Kennedy—an opportunity to show off personal qualities to maximum advantage. In the era of the captive mass public, from the 1950s through the '70s—when people had access to only a few TV channels, and the three national networks had a 90 percent share of the audience—the president had command of the airwaves, and the narrative of the evening news typically cast him as the dominant actor in the nation's daily political drama.

For a time, this seemed to be the permanent structure of the news and national politics in the age of electronic media. In retrospect, it was the peaking of the unified national public, the moment just before cable TV and the Internet began breaking it up, bringing the media to another historic turning point.

From the founding era to the late 20th century, the news in America enjoyed an expanding public. In the 1800s, postal policies and advances in printing technology cut the price of the printed word and, together with wider access to education, enabled more Americans to read newspapers and become civically literate. In the 20th century, radio, newsreels at the movies, and television extended the reach of the news even further.

The Advent of the Internet

It was only reasonable to assume, then, that the digital revolution would repeat the same pattern, and in some respects it has; online news is plentiful and (mostly) free. But a basic rule of communication is that abundance brings scarcity: an abundance of media creates a scarcity of attention. So although journalists and politicians have new ways to reach the public, the public has acquired even more ways to ignore them. Politics and other news are at our fingertips, but a lot of us don't want to go there. Between 1998 and 2008, according to surveys by the Pew Research Center, the number of Americans who say they don't get the news in any medium on an average day rose from 14 percent to 19 percent—and from 25 percent to 34 percent among 18-to-24-year-olds. And 2008 was a year when interest in the news should have been relatively high.

Obama's success in using digital media during the election may have led some to expect that as president he would be able to do the same. The job, however, is different. Rallying your activist base may not be the best way to win marginal votes in Congress. What Obama needs to do to win those votes—for example, make concessions to moderate Democrats on health-care legislation—may, in fact, disappoint his most passionate supporters. Mobilizing public support as president, rather than as a candidate, is also a different challenge. Although digital communications have made reaching political supporters cheaper and easier, the fractured nature of the public makes it more difficult to reach both the less politically interested and the partisan opposition.

Declining Viewership

During what the political scientists Matthew A. Baum and Samuel Kernell refer to as the "golden age of presidential television" in the early postwar decades, close to half the households in the country would watch a prime-time presidential TV appearance. As access to cable expanded in the 1980s, the audience started shrinking, and by 1995, only 6.5 percent of households watched one of Bill Clinton's news conferences. Obama started out with comparatively high ratings. According to [A.C.] Nielsen data, 31 percent of TV homes watched his first press conference, on February 9, [2009,] though that dropped to 16 percent by his fifth, on July 22. His speeches to Congress have drawn a somewhat bigger audience, but the ratings have followed the same trajectory. Nonetheless, the president still has the ability to command wider attention than any other figure in American politics. Obama's health-care speech to Congress on September 9 [2009] drew an estimated 32 million viewers, which was down from 52 million for his first address to Congress in February but still far higher than any other political figure could hope to attract.

After a summer when the national debate on health-care reform seemed to be dominated by his opponents—thanks, in no small measure, to Fox News and its one-sided coverage of protests at congressional representatives' town-hall meetings—Obama was able to reverse the momentum. In any conflict, the president's voice can rise above the noise. In any national crisis, eyes will still turn to the president, and citizens will expect him to speak for the nation. On those occasions, if he uses the opportunity well, he remains the country's most important teacher. And that remains Obama's greatest strength in competing with Fox over the direction of the national conversation.

Walter Cronkite

Cronkite was known for his journalistic objectivity. Unlike some of his contemporaries, Cronkite declined the opportunity to offer editorial commentary on the day's news, fearing that TV audiences would think that the entire newscast was biased. Only once in his career did he give his opinion: after returning from a 1968 trip to South Vietnam during the Vietnam War. Then, in four *Evening News* commentaries, he spoke out against the war. President Lyndon B. Johnson commented, "If I've lost Walter Cronkite, I've lost middle America." Shortly afterward, Johnson announced that he would not run for re-election.

Gale Biography in Context,
"Walter Cronkite," 2013.

A More Polarized Country

During his presidential campaign, Obama said he would try to repair America's bitter divisions, and he reached out to conservatives on various occasions, such as his visit to [televangelist] Rick Warren's Saddleback Church. American politics has become more polarized, however, for deep-seated historical reasons. With the shift of the South to the GOP [Republican Party], the Republicans have become a more purely conservative party, and the Democrats a more liberal one. If this change in the parties had occurred half a century ago, the dominant news media might have moderated polarizing tendencies because of their interest in appealing to a mass audience that crossed ideological lines. But the incentives have changed: on cable, talk radio, and the Internet, partisanship pays.

Not since the 19th century have presidents had to deal with partisan media of this kind, and even that comparison is imperfect. Today the media saturate everyday life far more fully than they did in early American history. Fox News, in particular, is in a league by itself. In the absence of clear national leadership in the Republican Party, Fox's commentators (together with Rush Limbaugh) have effectively taken over that role themselves. Although they have their liberal counterparts on MSNBC, the situation is not exactly symmetrical, because MSNBC's commentators do not have as strong a following, and the network's reporting is not as ideologically driven as Fox's.

The Future of Journalism

Of course, professional journalism, with its norms of detachment, hasn't disappeared, though it's in deep financial trouble. Leading newspapers, notably *The New York Times*, have a wider readership online and in print than they had before in print alone. Media-criticism blogs and Web sites from varied perspectives serve a policing function in the new world of public controversy. Partisan media are now firmly part of our national conversation, but countervailing forces—not just the political opposition and its supporters in the media, but professional journalists and other sources for authenticated facts—can keep partisanship from controlling that conversation. Although most American journalists assume that professionalism and partisanship are inherently incompatible, that is not necessarily so. Partisan media can, and in some countries do, observe professional standards in their presentation of the news. That is where civic groups and the scientific community, as well as media critics and others upholding those standards, should focus their pressure. Some commentators may be beyond embarrassment, but the news divisions of the partisan media are likely to be more sensitive to charges of unsubstantiated claims and loaded language. The yellow [sensationalistic, not-so-factual] press of the 1890s looked equally immune from rebuke—and for a long time it was—but the growth of professional journalism in the 20th century did bring about a significant degree of restraint, even in the tabloids.

No one can put the old public back together again. Walter Cronkite's death last July [2009] provoked nostalgia for a time when it seemed all Americans had someone they could trust, and that person was a journalist. But it's not just Cronkite that's gone; the world that made a Cronkite possible is dead. Now we have a fighting public sphere, which has some compensating virtues of its own. As in the early 19th century, a partisan press may be driving an increase in political involvement. After a long decline, voter turnout in the 2004 and 2008 elections returned to levels America hadn't seen in 40 years. Fox News and MSNBC stir up the emotions not just of their devoted viewers but of those who abhor them; liberals and conservatives alike may be more inclined to vote as a result. Democracy needs passion, and partisanship provides it. Journalism needs passion, too, though the passion should be for the truth. If we can encourage some adherence to professional standards in the world of partisan journalism, not via the government but by criticism and force of example, this republic of ours—thankfully no longer fragile—may yet flourish.

*"The new partisan press ... makes find-
ing [political] common ground seemingly impossible, or much more difficult."*

A Partisan Media Adds to Government Dysfunction

James L. Baughman

*James L. Baughman is an author and professor at the University
of Wisconsin Journalism School. In the following viewpoint, he
delineates the role of partisan journalism in US history and
traces its rise in the late twentieth century. Baughman asserts
that as the American public became more politically partisan in
the late 1960s, journalism also became more interpretive and
partisan in nature. Cable TV, political talk radio, and the Internet, he says, only intensified the divide. He argues that although
popular partisan media outlets are not a threat to the American
political system, they can obstruct the government's ability to
find consensus on a number of serious political, economic, and
social issues that America will have to confront in the next few
years.*

James L. Baughman, "The Fall and Rise of Partisan Journalism," Center for Journalism
Ethics, School of Journalism and Mass Communication, April 20, 2011. Copyright ©
2011 by the Center for Journalism Ethics, School of Journalism and Mass Communication. All rights reserved. Reproduced by permission.

As you read, consider the following questions:

1. According to Baughman, what was voter turnout in 1856?

2. According to a 2009 Pew Research Center poll cited by the author, what percentage of the American public believes the news media is politically biased?

3. When did Roger Ailes found Fox News, according to Baughman?

You don't need to have a degree in history—or even to have paid much attention when you suffered the US history survey course as an undergraduate—to know that American newspapers were very partisan in the 19th century. "Editors," wrote one historian, "unabashedly shaped the news and their editorial comment to partisan purposes. They sought to convert the doubters, recover the wavering, and hold the committed. 'The power of the press,' one journalist candidly explained, 'consists not in its logic or eloquence, but in its ability to *manufacture* facts, or to give coloring to facts that have occurred.'"

Party newspapers gave one-sided versions of the news. Papers in opposition to Andrew Jackson in 1828 attacked him for marrying a woman before her divorce had been finalized. He was the violator of marital virtue, a seducer. Jackson, one paper declared, "tore from a husband the wife of his bosom." Pro-Jackson newspapers insisted on the general's innocence, and accused his critics of violating his privacy. There was no objective, middle ground.

Stories that might flatter the opposition went unreported—or under-reported. As one historian observed, "The truth was not suppressed. It was simply hard to get in any one place." When Democrat Grover Cleveland won the presidency in 1884, the Republican *Los Angeles Times* simply failed to report this unhappy result for several days.

The Role of Economics in Media

Newspaper economics partly explained why, as one veteran editor observed in 1873, the press "was bound to party." Before the Civil War, parties actually subsidized the operations of many newspapers. Sometimes directly, sometimes through government printing contracts. In many cases, the subsidies were indirect and unknown to readers. Editors or their reporters worked part time for state legislators or members of Congress. Some of these relationships continued late into the 19th century. Needless to say, they were not terribly ethical.

Journalism historians, including our School's [University of Wisconsin's Journalism School] founder, Willard Bleyer, regarded the party press as a bad thing. Bleyer fervently believed newspapers had an obligation to educate the citizenry on matters of public policy. A biased news medium was bad for a self-governing people.

The Impact of Partisan Media

Although Bleyer reflected the views of several generations of journalism historians, more recent work has broken with this consensus. [University of Washington journalism professor] Gerald Baldasty and others argue that the party papers encouraged democratic participation, that they treated readers as citizens and voters, not passive observers. Declared the Worchester (Mass.) *Spy* in 1832, "Go to the polls [and] see that your neighbor goes there and vote for the men who have always been faithful to you and your interests." And voter turnouts, especially in the northern states, reached record levels, over 80 percent in 1856.

The more objective, detached journalists that Bleyer favored may have done their job *too* well. By examining politicians too closely, [Princeton economist] Thomas C. Leonard suggests, the press left the voter feeling helpless, even cynical, regarding the electoral process. Why bother? The percentage of voters turning out for elections dropped sharply in the

20th century; that is, once most newspapers ceased being party organs. *An average of about 60 percent voted in the last three presidential elections.*

At the same time, scholars like Baldasty maintain that the decline of the partisan press is not explained, as Bleyer would have hoped, by a more responsible, professional attitude among journalists and editors, many trained in new schools of journalism at [UW–]Madison and elsewhere.

Baldasty contends that *commercial* factors encouraged many newspapers to become less partisan. The cost of publishing a daily paper, especially in the largest cities, began growing to the point that party subsidies no longer covered operating costs. Even more, the presence of new revenue sources, specifically department stores and other retailers, more than made up for old party subsidies. Yet these new advertisers all but insisted that editors expand their reach, and be less partisan.

Such considerations drove most, though not all, newspapers to present the news more objectively. Newspapers did not march in lock step, especially in the 1930s, when the *Chicago Tribune* made no effort to disguise its distaste for Franklin Roosevelt. There were other holdouts, including, for many years, the *Los Angeles Times*.

The Rise of the Independent Press

Still, I would argue that by the 1950s most newspapers, large and small, as well as the broadcast networks, tried to present the news objectivity. What factors, in effect, closed the deal? The relative neutrality of broadcast journalists was explained in large measure by federal regulations that all but mandated fairness. But there are other explanations as to why our national news culture, whether print or broadcast, preferred the middle ground.

The middle ground was more populated. By that I mean that partisanship in the 1950s was less intense. This was in some degree because the Cold War had created a consensus on foreign policy, and much of the Republican party had accepted the outlines of the welfare state created in the 1930s. Even Robert A. Taft, the Republican Senate leader detractors said had the best 19th-century mind in the upper chamber, favored federal housing programs.

"Old Party divisions are less meaningful," wrote one *Fortune* magazine writer in 1960. "American political debate is increasingly conducted in a bland, even-tempered atmosphere and extremists of any kind are becoming rare." The differences were often subtle, having less to do with ideology than life style. One journalist told the political scientist Clinton Rossiter that you could tell the Democrats at a Rotary lunch. Their "dress is more casual, salutes are more boisterous, jokes are more earthy." As to Republicans, a friend growing up in suburban Milwaukee in the 1950s recalled, "I was led to understand that the way to tell a Republican household was that it owned a martini pitcher."

A Growing Divide

In the late 1960s and 1970s we began to see a greater division among our two major political parties. The Vietnam War fractured the Cold War consensus, mainly among more liberal Democrats. We had a much more active debate about fundamentals of US foreign policy.

At the same time, conservatives slowly became *more* conservative, and began to increase their influence within the Republican party. Moderate Republicans as a species all but vanished. A more conservative Republican party challenged some of the premises of the welfare state (and more recently, labor policies), as well as progressive income tax rates.

At the same time, mainstream news media (larger metropolitan daily papers and networks news) lost some if not much of their authority. Part of that loss was due to a change in what constituted objective news presentation. This is something [Canadian journalism professor] Stephen Ward wrote about so ably in his first book [*The Invention of Journalism Ethics*, 2004]. Reporters were encouraged to add analysis into their stories. Such analytical reporting more often than not, I think, had a liberal centrist slant. Not hard liberal. Not [TV talk show host] Rachel Maddow liberal. Maybe "neo-liberal." Here, I draw on [Columbia University sociologist] Herbert Gans's classic study of four major news organizations [*Deciding What's News*, 1979].

Look at the The New York Times in 1960 vs. 2010. The reportage is more interpretive [in 2010]. This is not a problem for me, but it is an issue for my more conservative friends (and I have them). The more analytical journalism could be off-putting for those on the fringes, left and especially on the right. One reader's analysis is another reader's opinion. Sixty percent of those surveyed by the Pew Research Center in 2009 believed reporting was politically biased.

There is a related problem that editors note and I encountered when I gave public service talks as director of the journalism school. . . . a lot of people can't distinguish the editorial page from the rest of the paper. Some assume the worst, that the editorial views of the newspaper inform the rest of the paper.

Media Failures

Various missteps by the mainstream media did not help.

- For many of those opposed to the Iraq war, *New York Times'* mishandling of claims that [Iraqi dictator Saddam] Hussein had WMD [weapons of mass destruction] in 2003.

- For Republicans in 2004, the flaws in CBS News's reports about President [George W.] Bush's military service during the Vietnam War.

News organizations have always made mistakes, but they have greater consequences when the consumers *have somewhere else to go. A safe harbor.*

Safe harbors became visible in 1987, when the end of the FCC's [Federal Communications Commission's] Fairness Doctrine empowered [controversial conservative talk show host] Rush Limbaugh and a much more opinionated talk radio. Then, in 1996, came Fox News, soon followed by the Internet, with web sites and blogs. All provided conservatives safe harbors for their world views.

There were safe harbors as well for those holding more liberal views, if we look at *Huffington Post* a few years ago or substitute MSNBC for Fox.

The Dominance of Independents

Has partisan journalism returned? Yes, but only in part. We need to remember that most Americans don't watch Fox News or MSNBC. Limbaugh claims to have the largest audience of any radio host. But most Americans on a given day do not listen to his program or view [fellow conservative host] Glenn Beck. Most Americans are *not* fierce partisans. Independents are the largest block of voters.

Let's look at the numbers. Much has been made of the declining popularity of the network evening newscasts. Katie Couric, anchor of *The CBS Evening News*, has had a particularly rough few years. Her newscast reached what the *New York Times* reported Monday [in April 2011] as "a record low" of 4.89 million viewers last August. Well, according to the Pew Research Center, Couric still drew roughly a third more viewers than [Fox News's] *The O'Reilly Factor*, and nearly four times what Keith Olbermann's *Countdown* averaged in 2010.

More Political Engagement

Although the audiences for the new party press should not be exaggerated, we should acknowledge that its fans are more likely to be politically engaged. Or, as [author and academic]

Louis Menand wrote in 2009, "people who need an ideological fix." The new partisan media can inspire or simply reassure those resting on the ideological fringes. If you belong to the Tea Party, you have Glenn Beck. If you think [conservative industrialists] the Koch Brothers are trying to purchase the State of Wisconsin, you have [liberal host] Ed Schultz.

You have a safe harbor.

So have we gone full circle? Is it 1850 all over again? I think not. Perhaps not even half way.

In contrast to the factious newspaper culture of the mid-19th century, today's media culture is in fact divided between the new partisan media of the radio, internet and cable, and those news outlets that still endeavor to report the news seriously. Serious news services won't, for example, provide platforms for those who insist the President was born in Kenya, or that the [George W.] Bush administration was behind the destruction of the World Trade Center.

As I noted, the serious or adult journalists still have the larger audience. But can they keep it? And, more to the point, does that larger audience really pay the freight?

Reporting vs. Opining

Roger Ailes brilliantly understood this when he founded Fox News in 1996. Ailes anticipated an argument that [Penn journalism professor] Joseph Turow made a year later that the media business model was changing. Advertisers, who had once pressed newspaper publishers to cover a mass audience, were now in search of niche audiences. The successful media entrepreneur, whether publishing a magazine or creating a cable channel, went after sub-groups of readers or viewers. In the case of Fox News, cultivating a niche audience of 60-something conservatives.

Ailes also recognized that news-gathering is far more expensive than opinion-spouting. It is far cheaper to produce a show from New York than to send reporters, like the Center's very own and gifted Anthony Shadid, into harm's way. And consumers of cable news understand this difference as well, when France, Britain and the United States launched air strikes against Libya several weeks ago, viewers turned to CNN, not Fox. (Alas, we cannot count on new military interventions to prop up CNN's ratings.)

Should everyone remain calm? After all, America survived the fiercely partisan press of the 19th century. But just barely. The robustness of political engagement then could not prevent the Civil War, and eliminate slavery peaceably. I am not so sure that Bleyer and others were so wrong to condemn the party press.

As in the 1850s, Americans have to make tough decisions. Not ones, fortunately, involving something as evil as slavery, but still difficult choices about our future. Fiscal crises on the state and national level require some compromise, the finding of common ground. The new partisan press, consumed so lustily by party activists, makes finding that common ground seemingly impossible, or much more difficult than it was a half century ago. And our political culture, as in the 1850s, has become deeply dysfunctional.

Periodical and Internet Sources Bibliography

The following articles have been selected to supplement the diverse views presented in this chapter.

L. Brent Bozell III	"A Dreadful Media Campaign," Media Research Center, November 6, 2012. www.mrc.org.
Mona Charen	"The Obama Press Votes Early," *Real Clear Politics*, September 25, 2012.
Ross Douthat	"The Media Bias That Matters," *New York Times*, September 27, 2012.
First Amendment Center	"The Myth of 'Media Bias,'" June 3, 2010.
Frank J. Fleming	"It's Media Love—Not Bias," *New York Post*, November 8, 2011.
Charles H. Green	"Trust in Media Down: Bias? Or Paranoia?" *Huffington Post*, September 25, 2012.
Kevin A. Hassett	"Who Is Really on the March?" *National Review*, November 2, 2010.
Robert Stacy McCain	"Whatever Happened to Truth?" *American Spectator*, October 3, 2012.
John Podhoretz	"Why Bam Can't Gaffe," *New York Post*, September 25, 2012.
Chuck Raasch	"A Fresh Case for Non-Partisan Media," *USA Today*, February 7, 2011.
Paul Rolly	"Partisan Media Dividing the Country," *Salt Lake Tribune*, August 11, 2012.
John Stoehr	"The Media Bias No One Talks About," *Huffington Post*, November 22, 2011.

OPPOSING
VIEWPOINTS®
SERIES

CHAPTER 3

How Do the Media Affect Society?

Chapter Preface

Iran's nuclear capability has been a matter of serious international concern for the past decade. Intelligence sources report that Iran is trying to develop a nuclear weapon that could threaten many of its enemies, especially Israel. Although Iranian officials contend that its nuclear program is being developed for peaceful civilian and environmental purposes—to generate electricity and lessen dependence on fossil fuels—intelligence officials believe that Iran is determined to build a destructive nuclear weapon that could decimate entire cities and kill millions of people.

Iran's nuclear aspirations have created conflict with many other governments. Both the United Nations (UN) and the United States have imposed economic sanctions and export controls on Iran in an attempt to discourage further development of nuclear weapons and force the country's leaders to accept more international oversight of its nuclear program. Despite harsh sanctions, Iran has remained adamant: it will not abandon its nuclear activities.

The situation worsened in November 2011. With mounting evidence that Iran had undertaken research and experiments geared to developing a nuclear weapon capability, the International Atomic Energy Agency (IAEA) board of governors censured Iran. This move prompted threats from Iran, who deemed the charges false and threatened to reduce its cooperation with the IAEA, the international body that provides oversight of nuclear programs in countries all over the world.

With the grim threat of Iran's advancing nuclear weapon capability looming, many countries began to seriously consider the idea of a military strike on the country's nuclear facilities. The main instigator of these threats is Israel, who fervently believes that a military strike against Iran may be necessary to defend itself. Many foreign policy experts think that Israel has a very good reason to believe that, because Iran has made no bones about its wish for Israel to be obliterated and wiped off the map completely. By 2011 it was looking more and more likely that a limited strike against Iran's nuclear facilities might be necessary to protect Israel and other nations from the dangers of a radical regime with nuclear power.

However, convincing the American people that an attack on Iran was necessary would be a challenging task. Public opinion polls were showing that Americans had mixed feelings about another military action overseas. To sway the public, politicians and pundits began to lobby: some to urge action, others to warn against any kind of military move.

Another player in the public relations battle was the press. Some journalists and commentators favored action and expressed that opinion. Others, who did not, underlined the need to stick with diplomatic solutions. In an atmosphere already mistrustful of the mainstream media, such a hot-button issue predictably caused more rancor and suspicion. Many began to question the role of the press in shaping public opinion on such an important matter and pointed to recent failures of the American press, particularly its performance during the run-up to the Iraq War. For many, the press had become a partisan player in a very serious situation.

The role of the news media in shaping public opinion is one of the topics explored in the following chapter, which deals with how the media affects society. Other viewpoints in the chapter debate media consolidation and the problem of movie violence and its relationship to societal violence.

> "Violent films and the packaging sur-
> rounding them seem both to reflect and
> to stoke the violence afoot in our land
> today."

Movie Violence Chic

Michael Massing

Michael Massing is an author, media critic, and contributing editor to the Columbia Journalism Review. *In the following viewpoint, he investigates the ways in which major movie reviewers have analyzed the connection between movie and societal violence in their reviews of the Batman movie* The Dark Knight Rises. *Considering that the Aurora, Colorado, movie theater massacre occurred at a midnight screening of the movie, Massing believes that there is little commentary on a possible link between the violence in the movie and the carnage in the theater, which he attributes to power of the Hollywood public relations machine. Massing argues that it is essential to recognize that violent movies not only reflect societal violence, but that they stoke both physical violence and the harshness of contemporary American public discourse.*

As you read, consider the following questions:

1. According to Massing, what three movie trailers disgusted him?

2. What did reviewer Anthony Lane say about the promotional campaign that accompanied *The Dark Knight Rises*, according to the author?

3. According to Massing, what film website had to suspend its user comments after some users threatened movie critics who had given a negative review to *The Dark Knight Rises*?

In recent weeks [as of July 2012], while watching baseball games, *The Daily Show*, and (I admit) some *Seinfeld* reruns, I saw what seemed a never-ending reel of trailers for *The Dark Knight Rises*, *The Amazing Spider-Man*, and *Savages*. And I became disgusted by the wall-to-wall violence in them—by the countless scenes of shootings and slashings, explosions and car crashes. Such interminable images of violence broadcast at all hours to a general audience could, I thought, only have a warping effect on society.

Then came the massacre in Aurora [Colorado] at the screening of *Dark Knight* on July 20 [2012]. In response, there's been the usual tide of commentary about the mindset of the murderer and the source of his weapons. These are of course important questions, and the revisitation of the madness of our gun laws is especially welcome. But I've been struck by how little attention has been paid to the movie itself. Among the news outlets I followed (including *The New York Times*, *The Washington Post*, and [National Public Radio's] *All Things Considered*), *The New Yorker* [magazine] was one of the few that really grappled with whether there might be a link between the violence in the movie and the carnage in the theater. [*New Yorker* film critic] Anthony Lane rejected such a link, flatly asserting that "no film makes you kill." Disagreeing,

[*New Yorker* film critic] David Denby argued that violence on the screen inures [hardens] us to actual violence. In forgetting that violence causes pain and death, we become "connoisseurs of spectacle." Denby expressed special concern for the ironic, detached attitude toward on-screen violence that has captured the smart set:

> The sophisticated response to movie violence that has dominated the discussion for years should now seem inadequate and evasive. An acceptance of dissociated responses as normal should not be the best we're capable of. Movies may never change, but we can change.

After the massacre, I went back and read the review of *The Dark Knight Rises* in *The New York Times*, and it illustrates what Denby is talking about. Manohla Dargis's references to violence are knowing, urbane, and highly attentive to style. "In a formally bravura, disturbingly visceral sequence that clarifies the stakes," she writes of the film's villain, "Bane stands before a prison and, in a film with several references to the brutal excesses of the French Revolution," delivers "an apocalyptic speech worthy of Robespierre." She added, "If this image of violent revolt resonates strongly, it's due to Mr. Nolan's kinetic filmmaking in a scene that pulses with realism and to the primal fear that the people could at any moment . . . become the mob that drags the rest of us into chaos."

I was struck, too, by the play the *Times* gave her review. It covered much of the front page of Friday's WeekendArts section, with a giant photo of Batman filling the right-hand side; the review's jump on page eight, which included a still from the movie, took up another half page. Sandwiched in between was a full-page ad for the film (with a blurb from *Newsweek* blaring at the top, "A Monumental Conclusion to the Epic Trilogy. Audiences Will be Blown Away").

It's hard to imagine that there's no connection between the space the *Times* gave its review (which was very positive) and the advertising for it. Hollywood is a huge source of revenue for the *Times*, and the paper compliantly gives blockbuster treatment to blockbuster movies. Both *The Amazing Spider-Man* and *Savages* got equally prominent review coverage, and both movies had large ads in the paper. The advertising does not guarantee a positive review—Dargis's review of *Spider-Man* was anything but—but it does seem to assure prominent and respectful treatment.

That treatment almost never involves discussing the level and nature of violence in these movies in any but an ironic, technical, and detached way. It's all about cinematography, visual effect, sequencing. In both its movie reviews and its many articles on the movie business, the *Times* rarely stops to consider the effects all this violence might have on the minds of individual moviegoers or on the national psyche as a whole. All of that advertising, I think, has the effect of co-opting the paper and making it a tacit (though, as I said, not always uncritical) arm of the movie industry, in which these types of issues are deemed either irrelevant or uncool.

The *Times* is not the only publication doing this. Anthony Lane's own review of the movie in *The New Yorker* falls into the violence-as-aesthetics camp. In his post on the Aurora massacre, however, he had some revealing things to say about the disturbing promotional campaign that accompanied the movie. It was not just a film, he noted; it "had become, as the studios like to say, and as the press is only too happy to echo, a 'movie event.'" Hence the midnight screenings all over the country and the well-advertised marathons that gave fans a chance to watch all three films in a row, the first two "raising the temperature of the third." It has been "a fever, of alarm-ing—and, we can now admit—foolish proportions. The fuss surrounding this movie did, and does, have something fevered and intemperate about it, something out of proportion to its nature."

In an arresting detail, Lane reported that, in the days before the film's release, the film website Rotten Tomatoes had to suspend its user comments:

> because the pitch of resentment, directed at critics who had dared to find the movie less than wonderful, had tipped into fury; Marshall Fine, of Hollywood and Fine, was told by readers that he should "die in a fire" or be beaten into a coma with a rubber hose.

Such aggression, Lane added, came from those who, by definition, could not yet have seen the film; they were watching the same trailers I was.

So, even apart from the question of whether the shooter was somehow affected by the violence in the movie, the fever stirred up by the marketing around the film created an atmosphere so nasty that commenters were calling for the death of a reviewer.

These violent films and the packaging surrounding them seem both to reflect and to stoke the violence afoot in our land today, and I'm not just talking about physical violence. The bombings, murders, and attacks on the screen, together with the marketing campaigns promoting them, seem inseparable from the ugliness of contemporary American discourse, with its anti-government extremists, raging talk show hosts, cable-news polemicists, fanatic gun lobbyists, angry xenophobes, and seething birthers [who believe President Obama was not born a US citizen]. That so few film reviewers and journalists covering the industry bother to explore such connections attests to the effectiveness and shrewdness of the Hollywood PR [public relations] machine.

"*[The] rise in fake [screen] violence may have played some role in the real-life trend heading squarely the other way.*"

There Will Not Be Blood

Charles Kenny

Charles Kenny is an author, a weekly columnist for the political journal Foreign Policy, *a senior fellow at the Center for Global Developments, and a fellow at the New America Foundation. In the following viewpoint, he analyzes the drop in US crime rates, as reported by the Federal Bureau of Investigation. Kenny maintains that these falling rates have a lot to do with a shift in cultural attitudes, as the United States becomes a more pacifist and tolerant society. He also contends that the trend toward more graphic violence on TV and in movies does not result in more societal violence but that, indeed, recent studies suggest that crime rates drop when violent blockbusters are playing at movie theaters. Kenny argues that these graphic movies seem to sate the bloodlust of American moviegoers.*

As you read, consider the following questions:

1. According to FBI statistics, as reported by Kenny, how many cases of violent crime were there per 100,000 US citizens in 2010?

2. How much did the proportion of people worldwide who say they would not want to have a neighbor of a different religion drop between the early 1990s and the mid-2000s, according to the author?

3. According to Gordon Dahl and Stefano Della Vigna, as cited by Kenny, violent movies deter how many assaults on an average weekend in the United States?

For all the grim news about the economy and jobs over the last few years, one indicator of the quality of life in the United States has stubbornly continued to improve. The latest Federal Bureau of Investigation data suggests crime rates went on falling through the first half of 2011, recession be damned. In 1991, the overall national violent crime rate reported by the FBI was 758 cases per 100,000 inhabitants; by 2010, that had dropped to 404 per 100,000. The murder and "nonnegligent homicide" rate dropped by more than half over the same period. You wouldn't know it from watching television—beyond the continuing conviction that "if it bleeds it leads" on local news, the number of violent acts on prime-time TV shows climbs ever upward. But that rise in fake violence may have played some role in the real-life trend heading squarely the other way.

The United States isn't alone in a trend towards people just getting along better—it's a global phenomenon. In 2001, homicide killed more than twice the number of people worldwide who died in wars (an estimated 557,000 people versus total war deaths of around 208,000). But just as in the United States, violent crime rates have been falling across a large part of the planet. The data is patchy, but in 2002, about 332,000 homicides from 94 countries around the globe were reported to the United Nations. By 2008, that had dropped to 289,000. And between those years, the homicide rate fell in 68 reporting countries and increased in only 26.

Look at the really long-term picture and violent crime rates are *way* down. Institute of Criminology professor Manuel Eisner reaches all the way back to the 13th century to report that typical homicide rates in Europe dropped from about 32 per 100,000 people in the Middle Ages down to 1.4 per 100,000 in the 20th century. (Sadly, of course, for all of their decline, U.S. rates are still more than three times that—a rate above what Eisner suggests is the Western average for the 1700s.)

The global picture of the last few years, along with the historical picture covering the West over the last 800 years, both suggest that there isn't just a constant proportion of bad people out there who will commit a crime unless you lock them up before they do it. And there's a lot more evidence that whatever is behind declining violence it isn't the number behind bars—or, indeed, the length of sentencing or the number of cops on the street.

It is true that a Pew Center report suggests that as U.S. crime rates were declining, the national prison population increased from 585,000 to 1.6 million between 1987 and 2007. But the rest of the world hasn't followed the United States down the path towards mass incarceration, and yet has still seen declining violence. The U.N. crime trends survey suggests that homicides fell in Britain by 29 percent between 2003 and 2008 alone, for example. And yet the incarceration rate in Britain was one-fifth as high as the United States, according to the Pew report. Again, within the United States, one of the places with the most dramatic drops in violent crime is New York City—the homicide rate is 80 percent down from 1990. But while the rest of the country was locking up ever more people, New York City's incarceration rate fell by 28 percent over the last two decades.

What about harsh punishment? Statistics from MIT psychologist Stephen Pinker's new book on global trends in violence show the United States used to execute more than 100

US Violent Crime Rate

Number of violent crimes (such as murder, non-negligent manslaughter, rape, robbery, and aggravated assault) committed in the United States per 1000,000 people from 1960 to 2008.

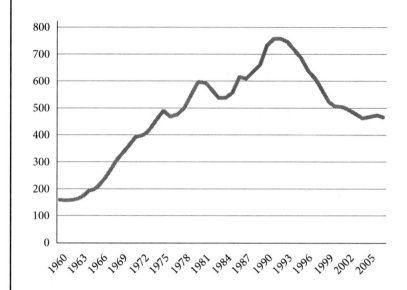

TAKEN FROM: Visconti, "Daily Graphic: US Violent Crime Rate, 1960–2008," *All That Natters*, May 20, 2009. http://allthatnatters.com.

times the amount of people in the 1600s as it does today—and yet violence rates then were far higher than today. Think Clint Eastwood's western, *The Good, the Bad and the Ugly*. Despite all of the authorized hangings, there was still a lot of unofficial shooting. More broadly, the number of countries using the death penalty has declined worldwide—along with violent crime rates.

In a survey asking "What Do Economists Know About Crime" for the National Bureau of Economic Research (NBER), Angela Dills, Jeffrey Miron, and Garrett Summers conclude "economists know little." They suggest that it isn't just incarceration or the death penalty—any link between lower crime and the number of police, higher arrest rates, and the stock of guns (whether more or less of them) is weak. Studies from Latin America have echoed that longer sentences are not linked to lower crime rates—although a higher probability of being caught may be related to less violence in the region.

At the same time, for those convinced that crime is a product of poverty and inequality, the recent trends for New York and the nation as a whole also pose a challenge: For all the growing estates of the plutocrats in Wall Street, neither growing inequality nor rising unemployment has reversed the downward path of crime. Similarly, Latin American evidence suggests that while rising inequality might be linked to increased violence in the region, average incomes are not—richer countries are no safer than poorer ones, all else being equal.

What about drugs, then? Interestingly, the NBER survey notes that drug enforcement might *increase* crime. The authors suggest that "If government forces a market underground, participants substitute violence for other dispute-resolution mechanisms"—i.e., if they can't go to court to settle their dispute over who gets which street corner, rival drug gangs will shoot each other instead.

New York's experience suggests that it is possible to reduce the violence associated with drugs by taking those disputes off of the street. Franklin Zimring, a law professor at the University of California, Berkeley, suggests that one important factor behind the decline in homicide in New York was shutting down open-air drug markets. It didn't slow sales, but it did eliminate 90 percent of drug-related killings over turf conflicts. Echoing the recent pattern in New York City, Eisner suggests that the long-term historical decline in Western homicide rates as a whole is associated with "a drop in male-to-male conflicts in public space."

Over the sweep of centuries, Eisner suggests that cultural change—from "knightly warrior societies" to "pacified court societies"—is an important factor. So are we just getting more civilized, then? Indeed, the decline in violence coincides with global evidence of converging attitudes towards greater toleration. For example, the proportion of people worldwide who say they wouldn't want to have a neighbor of a different religion dropped from 67 percent to 48 percent between the early 1990s and the mid-2000s. Turn on the television and you'd be sure to think that political dialogue is getting more rancid by the day. And it might be, but people's attitudes are actually becoming more pacific and tolerant.

Cultural factors are important, then. But before you rush to deride the Federal Communications Commission and the Supreme Court for their lackadaisical attitude toward violence on television, note that the trend toward more—and more graphic—violence on TV doesn't quite sync with the pattern of crime rates. A culture of violence and violence in popular culture are two very different things. In fact, one more element of cultural change that may behind declining violence is the substitution of fantasy violence for the real thing. French historian Robert Muchembeld argues in his book *History of Violence* that crime fiction and novels about war have given young men a way to indulge in violent fantasies without actually going out and stabbing someone. Or, over the last few years, they could stab someone playing *Grand Theft Auto* rather than stab someone while actually committing grand theft auto. This is the blood-and-gore version of the argument that more pornography leads to lower sexual violence.

There might be something to it. While exposing kids to the latest cadaver on *CSI*—or to Jack Bauer's lessons in successful torture on *24*—is probably a bad idea, watching an action movie might in fact reduce violence among adults. A recent study in the *Quarterly Journal of Economics* suggests that violent crime rates actually dropped when a blood-splattered blockbuster was in the cinema in the United States. The authors, Gordon Dahl and Stefano Della Vigna, looked at data from 1995 to 2004 and concluded that violent movies deter almost 1,000 assaults on an average weekend in the United States

Perhaps humanity will never completely abandon its lust for blood. But it appears that lust can in fact be sated using fake blood wielded by Hollywood special-effects technicians. And outside the theater, people respond to behavioral cues—if their friends don't stab people to win an argument, they are less likely to do it themselves. They also respond to institutional cues—if they can use the courts to settle a dispute or address a wrong, they're less likely to resort to blood feuds. All of which suggests the hope that, in years to come, there will be a lot more deaths on TV and movie screens than in the real world.

> *"If a handful of companies control the vast majority of what we constantly see, hear, and read about 24hrs a day, then the breadth of our information and democratic experience becomes considerably concentrated and narrowed."*

Media Consolidation Threatens Democracy and Free Speech

Ziad El-Hady

Ziad El-Hady is a writer and public speaker. In the following viewpoint, he argues that media consolidation is a troubling trend because it means that a handful of companies are controlling the flow of information and the interpretation of events. El-Hady maintains that this trend threatens democracy because the information the public needs to make informed and intelligent decisions about the leadership of the country and proposed policies becomes narrowed and manipulated. Media conglomerates concerned with the bottom line, he says, are happy to focus on celebrity news, sports, and scandals to gain readers, and will ignore nuanced, useful news stories. Another danger, El-Hady warns, is the political bias of media companies, which may favor candidates who will make them money or pass favored legislation. It is much better, the author concludes, to have a number of media sources that offer readers and viewers a range of information, opinion, and interpretations.

As you read, consider the following questions:

1. According to El-Hady, how many newspapers does Rupert Murdoch own worldwide?

2. What did researchers Greg Philo and Mike Berry find about media coverage of the Israeli-Palestinian conflict, as reported by the author?

3. According to Jack Shadeen, as cited by El-Hady, what percentage of Arab characters in Hollywood movies were negatively portrayed?

All social, political and economic policies and debates are communicated through our media. Therefore, the breadth of our democratic experience is largely defined by the structure of the media and its content. This may not be an immediate cause for panic in itself, but consider this alongside the centralisation of corporate media ownership and the picture becomes a lot more worrying. If a handful of companies control the vast majority of what we constantly see, hear, and read about 24hrs a day, then the breadth of our information and democratic experience becomes considerably concentrated and narrowed.

News does not come down to us raw and unadulterated. Rather, it is 'processed' and structured in terms of what topics are selected; how information is filtered; what is emphasised and what is ignored; how an issue is framed; and how a debate is bounded. Such tailoring gives Western news a specific 'character' to which we have all become innately accustomed.

As author of *The Press and Foreign Policy* (1993) Bernard Cohen points out, it's not so much that the media tells you what to think, it's that they tell you what to think *about*. Rupert Murdoch's News Corporation, for example, holds in excess of 130 newspapers worldwide, including the most widely circulated English newspaper in the world, *The Sun*. Now seeing as companies such as News Corporation are in competition with the likes of AOL, Murdoch's company will decide to turn many of these newspapers into profitable sensationalist journalism, focusing on the three themes of sex, crime, and sport.

Criteria for much news in general is about what can shock and rouse our emotions as opposed to what is actually informative and useful to society. Crime, sex/money scandals, bizarre/extremist opinions or behaviour, and *anything* to do with celebrities, occupies a large space within our mass media. Such attention-grabbing topics are also framed in ways that restrict our thinking even further. Violent crime reports, for example, take the form of concise horror stories, creating endless villains and victims out of our citizens rather than discussing the social problems that lead to such incidents. It's as if unemployment, inequality, poor education, and lack of moral sensitivity in society has nothing to do with such crimes. Our universities are, of course, filled with experts in such social sciences, but media professionals are largely uninterested in using their knowledge to create an intellectual platform to suggest ways in which we can minimise such offences in the future. Instead, politicians give simple solutions to appease the masses, while disregarding the opinions of experts. Moreover, there have been many studies which show that certain social problems, such as terror, violent and sexual crimes, have been exaggerated way out of proportion, while other studies show that more serious issues—many to do with the environment—are not emphasized enough or are completely ignored. Unsurprisingly, research shows that people who engage most with the mass media are more frightened of the outside world and have less trust for other people.

International Politics

The media also has a strong influence on people's political opinions due to the majority of sources coming from government and other establishment interests. [Social scientists] Edward Herman and Noam Chomsky extensively argue that in their book *Manufacturing Consent* (2002) that the modes of handling material by the mass media serve political ends and maintain existing political and corporate power structures. War is a typical concern for such thinkers. Political scientist Michael Parenti, for example, points out that "whenever the White House proposes an increase in military spending, press discussion is limited to how much more spending is needed . . . are we doing enough or need we do still more? No media exposure is given to those who hotly contest the already gargantuan arms budget in its totality". Typically, two choices are presented to the public but a third option that challenges the status quo is not.

There have been many studies that have analysed the political biases in the mass media, which are relevant to today's political climate. In a research-based publication, *Bad News from Israel* (2004) by Greg Philo and Mike Berry, the two-year study showed that the reporting of the Israeli-Palestinian conflict was biased towards Israel, which had significant effect on the attitudes and beliefs of Western audiences. The study showed, for example, that Israelis were interviewed or reported on more than twice as much as Palestinians, and Israeli casualties were strongly emphasised relative to Palestinians despite Palestinian casualties being greater in number. Even the language of news reports was used in such a way that favoured Israel. Words like 'hit-back' and 'retaliate' were used for Israeli action, while words like 'murder' and 'cold blood' were used for Palestinian action. There was also a lack of coverage on the context of the situation. That is, the forced mass evacuation of Palestinians from their homes, and a history of ethnic occupation, which, when not mentioned, makes the Palestinians look like they are initiating attacks for no reason.

Missing Context

Contextual details are typically neglected in such reports because essential root causes are seen as far less interesting than more shocking superficial symptoms. French sociologist and philosopher Pierre Bourdieu captures this point well when he describes news as "a series of apparently absurd stories that all end up looking the same, endless parades of poverty-stricken countries, sequences of events that, having appeared with no explanation, will disappear with no solution—Zaire today, Bosnia yesterday, the Congo tomorrow." Importantly, such social and political simplification or manipulation works contrary to the democratic goal of educating people.

Biased narratives in the film industry are far less subtle. In his book and documentary *Reel Bad Arabs: How Hollywood Vilifies a People* (2004), Jack Shaheen shows that Hollywood has vilified and portrayed Arabs as sub-human, militant, and barbaric to the masses since the beginning of film. In his research of over 1000 films that involved Arab characters or references, he found that around 90% were negative, 1% were positive, and the rest were neutral. For Shaheen, such 'stereotyping has become so wide-spread that it has become invisible.' Similarly, social psychologist Sam Keen, creator of *Faces of the Enemy* claims, "you can hit an Arab free; they are free enemies, free villains—where you couldn't do it to a Jew or you can't do it to a black anymore." Such social scientists never fail to mention the clear political manipulation, which, throughout history, has been used by a variety of political regimes to construct vile, ferocious representations of their enemies to justify invasion, occupation, killing, torture, and social exclusion. The phenomenon of Islamophobia is a current case in point.

We may not be physically forced to comply with state interests as in a dictatorship, though the result is not dissimilar. The corporate race for mass media consumption is a phenomenon that we as citizens pay the price for, both financially, and psychologically, producing news that is generally negative, superficial, and punchy; hardly ever constructive, beneficial, or thought provoking. Of course, not every item within the media is necessarily shaped by such interests, and good, honest journalism does exist. But the relentless prevalence of social and political misrepresentations on our TVs, news papers, on-line, and on the big screen, is certainly enough for us to question the integrity of our cognitive freedom and the soundness of our democratic experience.

| "Media consolidation is no threat to free
| speech."

Big Government, Not Big Media, Threatens Free Speech

Don Watkins

Don Watkins is an author, a columnist for Forbes, *and a fellow at the Ayn Rand Institute. In the following viewpoint, he asserts that the trend toward media consolidation is the result of people exercising their right to free speech on a large scale and is not a threat to free speech. Therefore, he argues, any attempt to regulate it or break up media conglomerates is a violation of free speech and an attack by big government to silence the public. Watkins maintains that the real issue is choice—media critics are unhappy with the popularity of conservative media and are employing government restrictions to force people to get their news from inferior sources. In Watkins's view, critics of media consolidation are the true enemies of freedom.*

As you read, consider the following questions:

1. According to Watkins, who was President Obama's pick to be chairman of the Federal Communications Commission?

2. Who does the author identify as a favorite bogeyman of media consolidation critics?

3. What Internet blogger does Watkins identify as a media mogul who has succeeded without huge financial resources?

Self-appointed consumer watchdogs—including Obama's recent pick for FCC [Federal Communications Commission] chair, Julius Genachowski—have long complained about media consolidation. So it was no surprise that when the FCC recently loosened restrictions barring companies from owning a newspaper and TV station in the same city, these critics went apoplectic and are now urging the House to follow the Senate in blocking the measure.

Media consolidation supposedly threatens free speech. A few conglomerates, critics warn, have seized control of our media outlets, enabling these companies to shove a single "corporate-friendly" perspective down our throats. As Senator Byron Dorgan put it, "The free flow of information in this country is not accommodated by having fewer and fewer voices determine what is out there. . . . You have five or six corporate interests that determine what Americans can see, hear, and read."

Leave aside that Dorgan's comments are hard to take seriously in the age of the Internet: his position is still a fantasy. Media consolidation is no threat to free speech—it is the result of individuals exercising that right.

All speech requires control of material resources, whether by standing on a soapbox, starting a blog, running a newspaper ad, or buying a radio station. Media corporations simply do this on a larger scale.

Consider the critics' favorite bogeyman, News Corp. When Rupert Murdoch launched the company, he and his fellow shareholders pooled their wealth to create a communications platform capable of reaching millions. They further expanded their ability to communicate through mergers and acquisitions—that is, through media consolidation. As News Corp.'s owners, shareholders were able to exercise their freedom of speech by deciding what views their private property would (and wouldn't) be used to promote—the same way a blogger decides what ideas to champion on his blog. Like most other media companies, News Corp. even extended the use of its platforms to speakers from all over the ideological map—including opponents of media consolidation.

Do News Corp.'s resources give Murdoch an advantage when it comes to promoting his views? Absolutely. Free speech doesn't guarantee that everyone will have equal airtime, any more than free trade guarantees that every business will have the same amount of goods to trade. What it does guarantee is that everyone has the right to use his own property to speak his mind.

Some of today's most prominent voices, such as Matt Drudge, have succeeded without huge financial resources. But regardless of how large a media company grows, it can never—Dorgan's complaints notwithstanding—determine what media Americans consume. It must continually earn its audience. Fox News may be the leading news channel today, but if it doesn't produce shows people want to watch, it will have all the influence of ham radio. Just think of how newspapers and the big-three network news stations are losing audiences to Web-based sources.

Now consider the actual meaning of government restrictions on media ownership. The FCC is telling certain Americans that they cannot operate a printing press or its equivalent. Such restrictions cannot protect free speech—they are in fact violations of the right to free speech. There is no essential difference between smashing someone's printing press and threatening to fine and jail him if he uses one; either way, he can't use it to express his views.

Rupert Murdoch

In half a century, Australian-born Rupert Murdoch has built a worldwide media empire that astounds both his admirers and his many vociferous critics. The holdings of his News Corp. Ltd. include not only newspapers and magazines but also book publishing concerns, television stations, and a satellite cable channel. Murdoch's reign has spread from Australia to England to the United States and even includes an outpost in Hong Kong. He turns a mostly deaf ear to the voices of his detractors, who consider him a philistine and his publications sleazy. And he continues to thrive. In an article in *Fortune*, Thomas Moore asked his readers to "think of Rupert Murdoch as the Magellan of the Information Age, splashing ashore on one continent after another. The natives laugh at him, they throw stones, and sometimes they give him gifts."

Gale Biography in Context, *"Rupert Murdoch,"* 2013.

What galls critics of media consolidation is not that News Corp. stops anyone from speaking—it's that they don't like the choices Americans make when free speech is protected. In the words of one critic: "[M]arket forces provide neither adequate incentives to produce the high quality media product, nor adequate incentives to distribute sufficient amounts of diverse content necessary to meet consumer and citizen needs." Translation: *Can you believe what those stupid consumers willingly pay for? If I got to decide what Americans watched, read, and listened to, things would be different.*

In order to "correct" the choices Americans make, these critics demand that the FCC violate the free speech rights of some speakers in order to prop up other speakers who, absent such favors, would be unable to earn an audience. In short, they want a gun-wielding Uncle Sam—not the voluntary choices of free individuals—to determine who can speak and therefore who *you* can listen to.

The critics of media consolidation are frauds. They are not defenders of free speech—they are dangerous enemies of that freedom.

Periodical and Internet Sources Bibliography

The following articles have been selected to supplement the diverse views presented in this chapter.

Michael J. Copps	"Protect Democracy by Fighting Media Consolidation," *Seattle Times*, January 3, 2013.
LZ Granderson	"Despite Newtown, We Crave Violent Movies," CNN.com, January 13, 2013. www.cnn.com.
Ann Hornaday	"Are Filmgoers Finally Rejecting Film Violence?," *Los Angeles Times*, February 7, 2013.
Steve Lendman	"Neocon Uber-Hawks Want War on Iran," *SteveLendmanBlog*, October 2, 2012. http://sjlendman.blogspot.com.
Brian Lowry	"Media-Ownership Rules Need New Look," *Chicago Tribune*, December 3, 2012.
Stephen Marche	"Don't Blame the Movie, but Don't Ignore It Either," *New York Times*, July 26, 2012.
Bernie Sanders and Michael Copps	"FCC Rule Change Would Favor Big Media," *Politico*, December 18, 2012.
Joe Satran	"'Dark Knight' Shooting Renews Question of Violent Movie Impact," *Huffington Post*, July 20, 2012.
David Sirota	"War with Iran: The Spin Begins," *Salon*, October 31, 2012. www.salon.com.
Kenneth Turan	"Does Violence in Film Lead to Real-Life Violence?," *Detroit Free Press*, July 20, 2012.
Steven Waldman	"How to Fix the Media Ownership Debate," *Columbia Journalism Review*, December 20, 2012.

OPPOSING
VIEWPOINTS®
SERIES

CHAPTER 4

What Is the Future of Mass Media?

Chapter Preface

In the past decade, live blogging has become a very popular method of news reporting. Unlike traditional news reports that summarize an event after its over—sometimes long after its over—live blogging reports breaking news as it happens. Reporters and editors employ it for its similarity to live television or live radio: Live blogging allows them to update stories continuously and in real time, providing the reader with the most up-to-date information on news events. For reporters on the scene of a news event, like the Arab Spring protests or the Super Bowl, the format allows them to provide running commentary and analysis from the scene and feature experts back in the newsroom. More than one reporter or analyst can weigh in on a live blog, and a number of multimedia elements—video, images, audio, Tweets and Facebook updates, and text—can be incorporated to provide further context for the story. Media experts praise live blogging for its ability to provide different layers of news coverage and analysis quickly. The format is used more and more frequently to cover sporting events, elections, protests and conflicts, and political and technology conventions.

According to a survey published by the City University London, live blogs are getting 300 percent more views and 233 percent more visitors than conventional online articles on the same subject. Readers access live blogs both as the news event is unfolding to get up-to-the-minute coverage and after the event is over. In the latter case, live blogging can become an archived, historical document that shows how the event unfolded and how perceptions of that news event developed and shifted during reporting.

One of the first major news organizations to use live blogging was the online edition of the British newspaper the *Guardian*. In 1999 it featured live coverage of soccer and cricket matches, which allowed sports reporters to provide running coverage of important matches and keep readers updated on every major play. In the United States, a number of technology websites were live-blogging web conferences and other technology events around the same time. On July 7, 2005, the *Guardian* used the format to cover the terrorist bombings in London's subway system, providing coverage from a stable of reporters in different venues. The *Guardian's*, success with live blogging inspired other online news organizations to follow suit. The format was widespread by the eruption of the Iranian protests in 2009, which provided minute-by-minute coverage as events occurred in a number of Iranian cities over a period of weeks. Live blogging had become one of the most popular ways to report breaking news.

The popularity of live blogging and its role in modern news reporting is one of the topics debated in the following chapter, which explores the future of mass media. Other viewpoints in the chapter discuss the role of Twitter in journalism, and the potential of social media and digital technology.

> "The mass-media era ... is coming to an end. ... A new generation that has grown up with digital tools is already devising extraordinary new things to do with them."

Social and Digital Media Are the New Mass Media

Economist

The Economist *is a weekly international news publication based in London. In the following viewpoint, the author traces the history of mass media and finds that it is coming full circle, back to its roots as a freewheeling and vibrant form. Centuries ago, the author reports, news traveled through social networks, until technology like the printing press allowed newsmakers to distribute pamphlets and newspapers to more people and across a larger area. However, the author explains, this technology also led to a few media moguls and companies taking control of the flow of information. With the advent of the Internet and social media, the author asserts, the social aspect of media has returned. Social and digital media, the author concludes, have facilitated a more diffuse flow of information and news and has undermined the traditional mass media model.*

As you read, consider the following questions:

1. According to the author, how did the Roman Empire disseminate important news and information?

2. How many religious pamphlets does the author estimate were printed and distributed during the time of Martin Luther?

3. According to Craig Newmark, as cited by *The Economist*, which three historical figures can be regarded as modern bloggers?

There is a great historical irony at the heart of the current transformation of news. The industry is being reshaped by technology—but by undermining the mass media's business models, that technology is in many ways returning the industry to the more vibrant, freewheeling and discursive ways of the pre-industrial era.

The History of Mass Media

Until the early 19th century there was no technology for disseminating news to large numbers of people in a short space of time. It travelled as people chatted in marketplaces and taverns or exchanged letters with their friends. This phenomenon can be traced back to Roman times, when members of the elite kept each other informed with a torrent of letters, transcriptions of speeches and copies of the *acta diurna* [daily deeds], the official gazette that was posted in the forum each day. News travelled along social networks because there was no other conduit.

The invention of the printing press meant that many copies of a document could be produced more quickly than before, but distribution still relied on personal connections. In early 1518 Martin Luther's writings spread around Germany in two weeks as they were carried from one town to the next. As Luther and his supporters argued with his opponents over

Rebels In Arms !

the following decade, more than 6m [6 million] religious pamphlets were sold in Germany. "News ballads", which spread news in the form of popular songs, covered the defeat of the Spanish Armada in 1588, among many other events.

In January 1776 Thomas Paine's pamphlet "Common Sense", which rallied the colonists against the British crown, was printed in a run of 1,000 copies. One of them reached George Washington, who was so impressed that he made American officers read extracts of Paine's work to their men. By July 1776 around 250,000 people had been exposed to Paine's ideas. Newspapers at the time had small, local circulations and were a mix of opinionated editorials, contributions from readers and items from other papers; there were no dedicated reporters. All these early media conveyed news, gossip, opinion and ideas within particular social circles or communities, with little distinction between producers and consumers of information. They were social media.

Rise and Fall of Mass Communications

The invention of the steam press in the early 19th century, and the emergence of mass-market newspapers such as the New York *Sun*, therefore marked a profound shift. The new technologies of mass dissemination could reach large numbers of people with unprecedented speed and efficiency, but put control of the flow of information into the hands of a select few. For the first time, vertical distribution of news, from a specialist elite to a general audience, had a decisive advantage over horizontal distribution among citizens. This trend accelerated with the advent of radio and television in the 20th century. New businesses grew up around these mass-media technologies. In modern media organisations, news is gathered by specialists and disseminated to a mass audience along with advertising, which helps to pay for the whole operation.

In the past decade the internet has disrupted this model and enabled the social aspect of media to reassert itself. In many ways news is going back to its pre-industrial form, but supercharged by the internet. Camera-phones and social media such as blogs, Facebook and Twitter may seem entirely new, but they echo the ways in which people used to collect, share and exchange information in the past. "Social media is nothing new, it's just more widespread now," says Craig Newmark. He likens John Locke, Thomas Paine and Benjamin Franklin to modern bloggers. "By 2020 the media and political landscapes will be very different, because people who are accustomed to power will be complemented by social networks in different forms." Julian Assange has said that WikiLeaks operates in the tradition of the radical pamphleteers of the English civil war who tried to "cast all the Mysteries and Secrets of Government" before the public.

News is also becoming more diverse as publishing tools become widely available, barriers to entry fall and new models become possible, as demonstrated by the astonishing rise of the *Huffington Post*, WikiLeaks and other newcomers in the past few years, not to mention millions of blogs. At the same time news is becoming more opinionated, polarised and partisan, as it used to be in the knockabout days of pamphleteering.

A Difficult Transition

Not surprisingly, the conventional news organisations that grew up in the past 170 years are having a lot of trouble adjusting. The mass-media era now looks like a relatively brief and anomalous period that is coming to an end. But it was long enough for several generations of journalists to grow up within it, so the laws of the mass media came to be seen as the laws of media in general, says Jay Rosen. "And when you've built your whole career on that, it isn't easy to say, 'well, actually, that was just a phase'. That's why a lot of us think that it's only going to be generational change that's going to solve this problem." A new generation that has grown up with digital tools is already devising extraordinary new things to do with them, rather than simply using them to preserve the old models. Some existing media organisations will survive the transition; many will not.

The biggest shift is that journalism is no longer the exclusive preserve of journalists. Ordinary people are playing a more active role in the news system, along with a host of technology firms, news start-ups and not-for-profit groups. Social media are certainly not a fad, and their impact is only just beginning to be felt. "It's everywhere—and it's going to be even more everywhere," says Arianna Huffington. Successful media organisations will be the ones that accept this new reality. They need to reorient themselves towards serving readers rather than advertisers, embrace social features and collaboration, get off political and moral high horses and stop trying to erect barriers around journalism to protect their position. The digital future of news has much in common with its chaotic, ink-stained past.

> *"Mobile is poised to surpass television as the dominant consumer access point for all media."*

Mobile Technology Is the Future of Media

Richard Ting

Richard Ting is the senior vice president and executive creative director of mobile and social platforms at R/GA, a digital advertising agency. In the following viewpoint, he contends that advertising is about to explode with the growth of mobile technology, particularly tablets and smart phones. Ting observes that there is a significant disparity between the consumer, who is increasingly turning to mobile technologies for his/her media fix, and advertisers, who still focus on traditional media sources. With mobile poised to surpass television as the consumer access point for all media, Ting asserts that consumers are entering the golden age of mobile technology.

As you read, consider the following questions:

1. According to Derek Thompson as cited by Ting, what percentage of their media attention are consumers spending on their mobile devices?

2. What percentage of an average person's time does the author estimate is used for noncommunication activities?

3. By how much does Ting say that globally "dumb-phone" users outnumber smart phone users?

This is the dawn of the smartphone age. But you wouldn't know it by looking at mobile advertising spend [monies spent on advertising]. Last week [end of May 2012] in this space, Derek Thompson showed that consumers are spending 10% of their media attention on their mobile devices while the medium only commands a mere 1% of total ad-spend. Comparatively, the quickly "dying" print medium attracts only about 7% of media-time, but still captures an astonishing 25% of the total U.S. ad-spend, with print receiving 25-times more ad money than mobile.

The disparity between the two mediums gives a strong indication as to how much room mobile still has to grow.

A Golden Age of Mobile Technology

While industry analysts have become increasingly bullish [optimistic] on the growth of the mobile medium and industry behemoths like Facebook are building out their mobile capabilities with the recent acquisitions of Instagram, Glancee, and Karma, it is perfectly clear that advertisers have avoided chasing consumers' eyeballs into this medium. While the ad-spend numbers don't quite match the perceived growth, a closer look shows us that we are actually beginning to enter the golden age of mobile and that the advertising spending will follow. To fully understand this trend, let's examine the features that characterize the rise of mobile today: its diversity, quality, innovation, experimentation, and cultural influence on society.

The diversity of tactics in the mobile medium is astounding. Advertisers now have an extremely robust palette of mobile

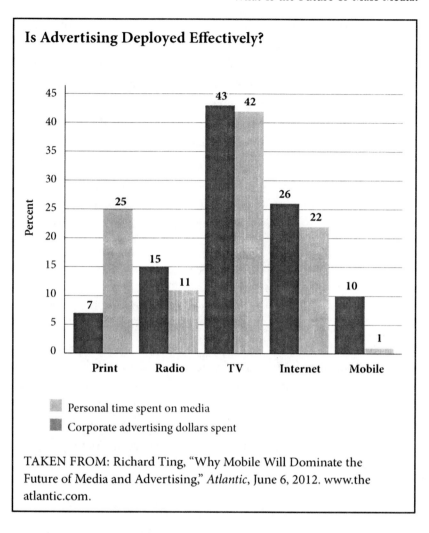

Is Advertising Deployed Effectively?

Personal time spent on media
Corporate advertising dollars spent

TAKEN FROM: Richard Ting, "Why Mobile Will Dominate the Future of Media and Advertising," *Atlantic*, June 6, 2012. www.the atlantic.com.

tools to choose from to connect their messages and experiences with their desired audiences thanks to advancements in mobile ad units, mobile search, mobile apps, mobile websites, and SMS [texting services]. Each of these mobile tactics is now being successfully embraced by advertisers to drive brand awareness, consideration, purchases, and loyalty.

Quality and Rapid Innovation

The quality of the work is at an all-time high. As a judge at the recent 2012 D&AD (Design and Art Direction) Awards, I received a strong overview of where the industry is heading and it's clear that some of the best creative and technical minds have finally shifted over to the mobile medium. Brands like Nike and their recent Nike+ Fuelband product shows just how far the quality of the work has come where the Nike+ Fuelband app leverages social platform design, Bluetooth integration, and 3D animations. This is a far cry from when mobile ad units were a brand's main mobile advertising option. The recent addition of the Mobile Lions to the Cannes Advertising Festival will also continue to accelerate this shift in talent and drive up the quality of mobile work in the upcoming years.

Innovation has accelerated. Recently, each innovative mobile product or service seems to beget the next one as the boundaries of the mobile medium continue to be stretched. In the past year, mobile has seen breakthroughs from the likes of Uber, Clear, Path, and Figure as mobile designers look to leverage location information, gestures, and UI [unit interval—i.e., transmission speed] advancements to reduce complexity and provide for more compelling services. In the near future, we'll also start to see more designers attempt to add voice control and personalization to improve users' experience on mobile.

Social Discovery Apps

Experimentation leads to advances. Recently, the apps Highlight and Sonar were released at SXSW [South by Southwest tech festival] with much fanfare. Both are considered social discovery apps, which help to monitor your location in the physical world and alert you when "similar" people are in close proximity to you. While, both of those apps have had difficulties gaining traction and overcoming the "creepy" label attached to them, they have fueled the imagination of what is now possible using a combination of GPS, open graph technologies, and the social web to find commonalities between people that were not always immediately obvious. Social discovery apps are leading the experimentation charge as the web evolves to become the 'personal web', a web rebuilt around individuals.

Cultural Influence on society. More than 2/3 of our time on mobile phones is now used for non-communication activities with the average American spending 94 minutes per day utilizing mobile apps vs. 72 minutes of web-based consumption. Mobile is poised to surpass television as the dominant consumer access point for all media. How we experience life, relationships, entertainment, education, exercise, and work have been completely transformed (for better or worse) because of mobile.

High Growth Potential

It's Still Only the First Inning. Despite mobile's progress and momentum, we're still only at the beginning of the golden age of mobile. There is still a huge gap between the rapid adoption of mobile and the budgets assigned to it. Brands will need to more than quadruple their mobile budgets to begin catching up to the level at which consumers are embracing the channel. Statistics also show that globally "dumb-phone" users still outnumber smartphone users 5.6 billion to 835 million, meaning that the "upgrade cycle" to smartphones is still in the early stages.

Imagine a world in the next 2–3 years, where smart phones are in the hands of every consumer and tablet sales will exceed PCs. It will be a world where global internet users will double, led by mobile usage. At that time, mobile will no longer be a support medium, it will be THE medium. Today, we've already seen apps disrupt multi-billion dollar industries—gaming, retail, media, publishing, small business, photography, and travel.

At this point, not having a mobile strategy/roadmap in place for your brand is a recipe for disruption. The golden age of mobile is here and will be here for years.

| "Rather than foretelling the death of journalism, the live blog is surely the embodiment of its future."

Live Blogging Is Transforming Journalism

Matt Wells

Matt Wells is the US blogs and networks editor at the Guardian, *a major newspaper and news service in the United Kingdom. In the following viewpoint, he delineates the benefits and the drawbacks of live blogging, arguing that despite its limitations and challenges there is a lot of hope for its future among news media leaders. A number of editors believe that the format of live blogging needs to be rethought in order to avoid confusion for readers and present information in a more organized manner, Wells explains. Despite the necessity of tweaking the format, Wells contends that live blogging has already become the dominant form for breaking news online and is profoundly transforming journalism.*

As you read, consider the following questions:

1. According to Wells, live blogs on the *Guardian*'s website accounted for how many unique users in March 2011?

2. What does Wells think one of the drawbacks was with live blogging the Arab Spring uprisings?

3. According to Benjamin Cohen, as cited by the author, what do live blogs need in order to work?

10.57 GMT [Greenwich Mean Time (the UK's time zone)] Hello and welcome to an article about live blogging, a discussion of a format that has been derided as murdering traditional reporting but is almost certainly the most important journalistic development of the past year. Unfortunately, it's impossible to sustain the live blog format beyond that opening conceit. Because that is the key point; live blogging is a uniquely digital format that has evolved in a way that is native to the web.

The Growth of Live Blogging

This year, as the Arab revolutions have unfolded, live blogging has rapidly become the dominant form for breaking news online—deployed by virtually every major news organisation on their home page and the online answer to 24/7 television news. The *Financial Times* has had to commandeer [its foreign affairs editor] Gideon Rachman's blog to keep up, while the styles vary from the quickfire updates of the BBC (complete with BBC News broadcast feed), to the tight and factual *Daily Telegraph* technique, to a slightly more expansive approach from the *Guardian*.

The reward is huge traffic spikes, hundreds of comments—so far in March [2011], live blogs (including minute-by-minute coverage of sporting events) on guardian.co.uk account for 3.6 million unique users, 9% of the total—and the wrath of some traditional readers who clamour for a straight-up-and-down, conventionally written article. One blogger even described live blogs as the "death of journalism".

What Is Live Blogging?

If you're attending a conference or other event related to your blog's niche, you might want to consider live blogging from the event. Live blogging is basically just posting regular updates to your blog as the event is taking place, rather than blogging about it after the fact.

Cameron Chapman, HongKiat.com, 2012. www.hongkiat.com.

Positive Aspects of Live Blogging

I should declare an interest. As the blogs editor of the *Guardian*, I am instinctively an enthusiast. They provide a useful way of telling stories characterised by incremental developments and multiple layers. They are open about the limitations of journalism and draw in the expertise of the audience—and even take input from journalists on rival publications.

On fast-moving stories, live blogs give the ability to post significant developments quickly—more quickly than editing and re-editing a news article. They also allow us to link out to other coverage, to include comments from Twitter and Facebook, to display multimedia (pictures, video and audio), and to include our audience in the comments below the line—all in one place. Neil McIntosh, the online editor of the *Wall Street Journal* Europe, says: "It's a form that's charming in its directness; at its best it generally does away with any writerly conceits, and demands the author just get on with telling you what's just happened."

Drawbacks of Live Blogging

But there are drawbacks: on stories without a defined timescale, such as the Arab Spring uprisings, live blogs can get long and confusing. Robert Mackey, who writes live news blogs for the *New York Times*, while clearly an advocate, warns: "You are more or less providing readers with raw material rather than telling them a story. You also tend to get swept up in the rush of events, and don't have nearly as much time as you'd like to think about what's happening and make connections, or write any sort of news analysis."

They require careful, continuous signposting to guide the reader to the story's main points. When comments run into the hundreds, they need curating and managing. If done badly, they can descend into a mishmash of tweets and comments without context.

They can be too easily deployed by editors on stories to which the format is not suited. And the name, live blogging, does not helpfully describe the format and suggests triviality.

The Potential of Live Blogging

Nevertheless editors are obviously confident about the format. Martin Belam, a web information architect who has worked at the BBC and is now at the *Guardian*, says: "It feels like a type of news reporting that is emerging as being native to the web. Most video news on the internet is essentially the same kind of package that you'd produce for TV, most audio the same as you'd produce for radio, and most text-based news could be printed out. The emerging live blog style isn't any of those things."

Benjamin Cohen, technology correspondent for [the UK's] Channel 4 News, says live blogs need "a lot of content" to work. "Liveblogging also really only works if you have a big enough audience to read and share it. But, you also get a similar experience on Facebook and Twitter. Sometimes it's more interesting to look at the Twitter stream of a breaking news story, and you don't need someone curating content and telling you what's important," Cohen adds.

"Live blogs don't work for everything, they give an instant reaction but they're not authenticated like website news stories. When it does work it makes web pages come to life."

Rethinking the Format

Almost everyone involved in live blogging sees the drawbacks. The potential for confusion, and the difficulty that users can encounter if they come across a live blog in the middle of a story, is clear.

The result is that some feel the format needs to be rethought. Kevin Anderson, a digital media consultant and former *Guardian* digital research editor, believes there should be more consideration given to the types of stories on which it is deployed. He says that news organisations "need to get smarter with how we present it", and argues that: "Curating news from multiple sources can't be just about speed and volume." Anderson's worry is that some live blogs are "just a jumbled stream of Twitter updates with no context as to who the people are, and no information about what their role or interest is in the story".

It is hard not to agree. The BBC has done an excellent job in reformatting its "live page" to include a permanent summary of the latest developments, and an easy link to the latest version of the conventionally written news story. The *Guardian* is rethinking how it presents the format too.

However, the best elements of live blogging—how it is so transparent about sources, how it dispenses with false journalistic fripperies and embraces the audience—are so strong that, rather than foretelling the death of journalism, the live blog is surely the embodiment of its future.

"[News] articles . . . are no longer necessary for every event. They were a necessary form for newspapers and news shows but not the free flow, the never-starting, never-ending stream of digital."

Twitter Is Transforming Journalism

Jeff Jarvis

Jeff Jarvis is a blogger, author, journalist, media consultant, and associate professor and director of the Tow-Knight Center for Entrepreneurial Journalism at the City University of New York's Graduate School of Journalism. In the following viewpoint, he maintains that social media, particularly Twitter, is transforming the way journalism is being practiced today. Twitter and other technologies allow journalists to focus on reporting events, interviewing witnesses, debunking rumors, and posting pictures and video in real time, he says. Jarvis contends Twitter and other technologies signal the decline of the long-form article, which provides a coherent narrative of complex events and provide essential context, but also takes time and resources to write and is often outdated by the time it is put together and published. In Jarvis's view, articles should be regarded as the by-product of journalism, not the goal of the entire process.

As you read, consider the following questions:

1. According to Jarvis, what *New York Times* reporter had his colleagues write a long story about the Joplin tornado from his tweets?

2. What journalist's tweets does the author single out as adding "tremendous journalistic value" to our understanding of the Arab Spring?

3. What qualities does Jarvis think that a journalist must have to thrive in this new media environment?

A few episodes in the news make me think of the article not as the goal of journalism but as a value-added luxury or as a byproduct of the process.

Twitter As Journalism

See the amazing Brian Stelter covering the Joplin tornado [a deadly tornado that hit Joplin, Missouri, in 2011] and begging his desk at *The [New York] Times* to turn his tweets into a story because he had neither the connectivity nor the time to do it in the field and, besides, he was too busy doing something more precious: reporting. (It's a great post, a look at a journalist remaking his craft. Highly recommended for journalists and journalism students particularly.) (And aren't you proud of me for not drawing the obvious and embarrassing comparison to *Times* editor Bill Keller's Luddite trolling about Twitter even as his man in Twitter, Stelter, proves what a valuable tool it is?)

In Canada's recent election, Postmedia (where—disclosure—I am an advisor) had its reporters on the bus do *nothing* but reporting, putting up posts and photos and videos and snippets as they went, keeping coverage going all day, maximizing their value in the field. Back at HQ [headquarters], a "twin" would turn that into a narrative—as blog posts—when appropriate. At the end of the day, the twin would also turn out a story for print, though everything had pretty much been done earlier; this was more an editing than a writing task. I asked my Postmedia friends what had to be done to turn the posts into an article. Mostly, they said, it meant adding background paragraphs (those great space-wasters that can now be rethought of as links to regularly updated background wikis, don't you think?).

Live Blogging

At South by Southwest [a big tech fair], the *Guardian*'s folks talked about their stellar live-blogging. Ian Katz, the deputy editor, said that live-blogging—devoting someone to a story all day—was expensive. I said that writing articles is also expensive. He agreed. There's the choice: Some news events (should we still be calling them stories?) are better told in process. Some need summing up as articles. That is an extra service to readers. A luxury, perhaps.

Twitter and the Arab Spring

Of course, I need to point to [National Public Radio's social media strategist] Andy Carvin's tweeting and retweeting of the Arab Spring. He adds tremendous journalistic value: finding the nodes and networks of reliable witnesses; questioning and vetting what they say; debunking rumors; adding perspective and context; assigning his audience tasks (translating, verifying a photos' location); even training witnesses and audiences (telling them what it really means to confirm a fact). What he does never results in an article.

A New Journalistic Process

I've been talking with some people about concepts for reorganizing news organizations around digital and I keep calling on [digital media executive] John Paton's goal to keep in the field and maximize the two things that add value—reporting and sales—and to make everything else more efficient through consolidation or outsourcing. As I was talking to someone else about this, it occurred to me that in some—not all—cases, not only editing and packaging but even writing could be done elsewhere, as Postmedia did in its election experiment. I'm not talking about complex stories from beat people who understand topics and need to write what they report from their earned understanding. I'm talking about covering an event or a meeting, for example. The coverage can come from a reporter and in some cases from witnesses' cameras and quotes. The story can be written elsewhere by someone who can add value by compiling perspectives and facts from many witnesses and sources. It harkens back to the days of newspaper rewritemen (I was one).

Carry this to the extreme—that's my specialty—and we see witnesses everywhere, some of them reporters, some people who happen to be at a news event before reporters arrive (and now we can reach them via Twitter, Facebook, Foursquare. . .), some who may be participants but are sharing photos and facts via Twitter. Already on the web, we see others—bloggers—turn these distributed snippets into narratives: posts, stories, articles.

The Future of Articles

The bigger question all this raises is when and whether we need articles. Oh, we still do. Articles can make it easy to catch up on a complex story; they make for easier reading than a string of disjointed facts; they pull together strands of a story and add perspective. Articles are wonderful. But they are no longer necessary for every event. They were a necessary form for newspapers and news shows but not the free flow, the never-starting, never-ending stream of digital. Sometimes, a quick update is sufficient; other times a collection of videos can do the trick. Other times, articles are good.

I've been yammering on for a few years about how news is a process more than a product. These episodes help focus what that kind of journalism will look like—and what the skills of the journalist should be.

The accepted wisdom of journalism and its schools was that storytelling was our real job, our high calling, our real art. Ain't necessarily so. The accepted wisdom of blogging has been that now any of us can do everything: report and write, producing text and audio and video and graphics and packaging and distributing it all. But I also see specialization returning with some people reporting, others packaging. Can we agree to a new accepted wisdom: that the most precious resource in news is reporting and so maximizing the acquisition of facts and answers is what we need?

Article As By-product

So what is an article? An article can be a byproduct of the process. When digital comes first and print last, then the article is something you need to put together to fill the paper; it's not the goal of the entire process. The process is the goal of the process: keeping the public constantly informed.

An article can be a luxury. When a story is complex and has been growing and changing, it is a great service to tie that into a cogent and concise narrative. But is that always necessary? Is it always the best way to inform? Can we always afford the time it takes to produce articles? Is writing articles the best use of scarce reporting resources?

In a do-what-you-do-best-and-link-to-the-rest ecosystem, if someone else has written a good article (or background wiki) isn't it often more efficient to link than to write? Isn't it more valuable to add reporting, filling in missing facts or correcting mistakes or adding perspectives, than to rewrite what someone else has already written?

We write articles for many reasons: because the form demands it, because we want the bylines and ego gratification, because we are competitive, because we had to. Now we should write articles when necessary.

The New Journalist

This new structure changes not only the skills but likely the character of the journalist. These days when I see young journalists talk only about their passion to write and tell stories, I worry for them that they will find fewer jobs and less of a calling. But when I hear journalists say that their passion is to report, to dig up facts, to serve and inform the community by all means possible, I feel better. When I hear a journalist talk about collaboration with that community as the highest art, then I get happy.

Let the record show that I am not declaring the article useless or dead. Just optional.

Postscript

Seconds after I posted this to Twitter, Chad Catacchio said that by the time the article is written, it's not news, it's history (albeit the fabled first draft).

If you came to this post via Mathew Ingram's response, please note that I adamantly disagree with his characterization of what I say. See my comment under Facebook comments at the end of his post.

LATER: Jonathan Glick has a smart take on this notion, arguing that nuggets of news will be delivered as nuggets, freeing journalists to write analyses, adding their value, without the burden of conveying the latest.

There is nothing sacred about the article for the transmission of news. It is a logical way of packaging information for a daily print run of a newspaper and a useful format around which to sell display advertising. It has survived into

What Is Twitter?

Twitter is a real-time information network that connects you to the latest stories, ideas, opinions and news about what you find interesting. Simply find the accounts you find most compelling and follow the conversations.

At the heart of Twitter are small bursts of information called Tweets. Each Tweet is 140 characters long, but don't let the small size fool you—you can discover a lot in a little space. You can see photos, videos and conversations directly in Tweets to get the whole story at a glance, and all in one place. . . .

You don't have to build a web page to surf the web, and you don't have to tweet to enjoy Twitter. Whether you tweet 100 times a day or never, you still have access to the voices and information surrounding all that interests you. You can contribute, or just listen in and retrieve up-to-the-second information. . . .

Twitter was founded in San Francisco, but it's used by people in nearly every country in the world. The service is available in more than 20 languages, and we continue to add them.

Twitter.com, 2013. https://twitter.com.

the Internet age for reasons of tradition and the absence of better formats. We have come to accept it as a fundamental atom of news communication, but it's not. Given faster, easier alternatives, the article no longer makes sense to mobile users for consuming news.

News will go one way, into the stream as scannable updates, and analysis will go the other, toward a new long-form business model for writers. I believe it will be a happy divorce.

I like his take except for this notion that journalism will be defined by length. I find "long-form" to be often used in a rather self-indulgent way: I want to write a lot, it says, and I want you to read it all. Now I know that's now what Glick is saying; he's saying that one must have a lot to say, a lot to add. But I think we need another way to describe that than by the inch, for I'm sure we've all known too many writers who like to write more than inform.

Amy Gahran has a very nice piece—not just because she agrees with me—whose subhead begins:

> The cutting room floor of journalism is a sad place: all those facts, interviews, asides, anecdotes, context, insights, and media gathered during reporting which, while relevant and interesting, just doesn't fit comfortably into the narrative flow or length/time limits of the finished story.
>
> This doesn't merely represent wasted time and reporting effort. Many of those scraps are missed opportunities to engage readers and gain search visibility or links . . .

Well-said. She argues that we need to look at assembling news the way we play with Legos and we need CMSes that will do that (Storify is a start).

Periodical and Internet Sources Bibliography

The following articles have been selected to supplement the diverse views presented in this chapter.

John Backus	"The Future of 'Television,'" *Huffington Post*, December 2, 2011. www.huffingtonpost.com.
Emily Bell	"Journalism by the Numbers," *Columbia Journalism Review*, September 5, 2012.
Jordan Friedman	"In Digital Age, Social Media Impacts College Journalism," *Huffington Post*, January 29, 2013. www.huffingtonpost.com.
Kira Goldenberg	"The Genuine Article," *Columbia Journalism Review*, September 5, 2012.
Matthew Ingram	"The Future of Media = Many Small Pieces, Loosely Joined," GIGAom, April 13, 2012. http://gigaom.com.
John Kass	"What Really Goes on at Tribune Tower," *Chicago Tribune*, October 20, 2010.
Allison Lee	"Blogging and Journalism: Not the Same Thing," *Punch*, July 17, 2012.
David Marsh	"Digital Age Rewrites the Role of Journalism," *Guardian* (Manchester, UK), October 16, 2012.
Adam Poltrack	"The Future of TV Content Delivery Is the Internet," *Digital Trends*, December 8, 2012.
Peter Preston	"The Future May Be Online, but Many Will Slip Through the Net," *Observer* (London), August 27, 2011.
Felix Salmon	"How Blogs Have Changed Journalism," Reuters, March 16, 2011. www.reuters.com.

For Further Discussion

Chapter 1

1. Should the news media be fact-checking the statements of presidential candidates and other politicians? Explain your answer citing from the viewpoints written by Brendan Nyhan, James Taranto, Jack Shafer, and Mark Hemingway to inform your response.

2. Juan Cole contends that the news media does a poor job of keeping readers and viewers apprised of important global events. Do you agree or disagree? How can your news media sources improve international coverage?

Chapter 2

1. Jonah Goldberg suggests that there is a liberal media bias. John Merline asserts that there is a conservative news bias. Paul Farhi argues that there is no significant news bias. Which view do you agree with and why?

2. In his viewpoint, L. Brent Bozell III maintains that the media influenced the 2012 presidential election. Eric Alterman contends that conservatives are trying to influence news coverage by charging bias. After reading both viewpoints, which author do you think makes the better argument? Why?

3. Partisan media has a long history in the United States. Reflect on your own attitude toward biased media sources. Do you think a partisan press inspires or depresses participation in the political process? Explain.

Chapter 3

1. Do you think that movie violence affects societal violence? Explain your answer citing from the viewpoints by Michael Massing and Charles Kenny to inform your answer.

2. Ziad El-Hady maintains that media consolidation is a threat to free speech and democracy. Don Watkins suggests that government interference in media consolidation is the true threat. What is your opinion on the matter? Cite from the viewpoints in your answer.

Chapter 4

1. How is journalism being revolutionized by social media, mobile technology, and live blogging? Cite from the viewpoints by *The Economist*, Richard Ting, Matt Wells, and Jeff Jarvis, but draw from your own experiences as well in your answer.

Organizations to Contact

The editors have compiled the following list of organizations concerned with the issues debated in this book. The descriptions are derived from materials provided by the organizations. All have publications or information available for interested readers. The list was compiled on the date of publication of the present volume; names, addresses, phone and fax numbers, and e-mail and Internet addresses may change. Be aware that many organizations take several weeks or longer to respond to inquiries, so allow as much time as possible.

Accuracy in Media (AIM)
4455 Connecticut Ave. NW, Ste. 330, Washington, DC   20008
(202) 364-4401 • fax: (202) 364-4098
e-mail: info@aim.org
website: www.aim.org

Accuracy in Media is "a non-profit, grassroots citizens' watchdog of the news media that critiques botched and bungled news stories and sets the record straight on important issues that have received slanted coverage." The organization finds examples of liberal media bias in print, television, and other media; provides an analysis of biased stories; counters misinformation and distortions; and coordinates media conferences, lectures, and symposia to discuss the subject of media bias and develop strategies to facilitate a more balanced US media. The AIM website features blogs, audio and video of speakers and experts, commentary, and special reports.

American Civil Liberties Union (ACLU)
125 Broad St., 18th Fl., New York, NY   10004
(212) 549-2500
website: www.aclu.org

The American Civil Liberties Union works to protect and extend the rights of all Americans, particularly equal protection under the law, the right to due process, the right to privacy, and First Amendment rights. The ACLU takes on the thorniest issues: racism, sexism, homophobia, religious intolerance, and censorship. It has often tangled with the Federal Communications Commission in order to push back against censorship and support free speech and free expression on television and the Internet. On the ACLU website, the group posts video, podcasts, games, documents, reports, and speech transcripts, as well news and commentary on censorship and free speech issues. The ACLU also offers a blog and in-depth reports on related issues.

Center for Media and Democracy (CMD)
520 University Ave., Ste. 260, Madison, WI   53703
(608) 260-9713 • fax: (608) 260-9714
website: www.prwatch.org

The Center for Media and Democracy is a nonprofit investigative group that exposes the ways in which the media is influenced by corporate spin and government propaganda. One of its recent investigations focused on the American Legislative Exchange Council (ALEC), a conservative group created to draft and advocate for business-friendly policies and legislation. The CMD website features in-depth reports on corporate media influence, campaign finance, the banking scandal, election fraud, and other pertinent subjects. It also offers updates on recent initiatives, breaking news, staff and guest commentary, a video archive, and access to *SPIN*, an e-newsletter.

Center for Media and Public Affairs (CMPA)
933 N. Kenmore St., Ste. 405, Arlington, VA   22201
(571) 319-0029 • fax: (571) 319-0034
e-mail: mail@cmpa.com
website: www.cmpa.com

Affiliated with George Mason University, the Center for Media and Public Affairs is an independent research and educational organization that provides "an empirical basis for ongoing debates over media coverage and impact through well-documented, timely, and readable studies." The CMPA emphasizes a scientific approach to media research, differentiating it from other media watchdog groups. One of CMPA's main efforts has focused on improving the election process. Recent studies, which are available on the CMPA website, include the use of political humor in media coverage and science and health reporting.

Fairness and Accuracy in Reporting (FAIR)

104 W. Twenty-Seventh St., Ste. 10-B, New York, NY   10001
(212) 633-6700 • fax: (212) 727-7668
e-mail: fair@fair.org
website: fair.org

Formed in 1986, the media watchdog group Fairness and Accuracy in Reporting documents examples of media bias, advocates for greater diversity in the press, amplifies neglected news stories and marginalized voices, and fights against censorship. FAIR "believes that structural reform is ultimately needed to break up the dominant news conglomerates, establish independent public broadcasting and promote strong non-profit sources of information." The FAIR website features a blog that provides analysis of recent media coverage on important events; *Counterspin*, the organization's weekly radio show and archives of earlier shows; and access to *Extra!*, FAIR's monthly magazine.

Federal Communications Commission (FCC)

445 Twelfth St. SW, Washington, DC   20554
(888) 225-5322 • fax: (866) 418-0232
e-mail: fccinfo@fcc.gov
website: www.fcc.gov

The Federal Communications Commission's stated directive is to regulate "interstate and international communications by radio, television, wire, satellite and cable in all 50 states, the District of Columbia and U.S. territories." On its website, the FCC indicates that it "was established by the Communications Act of 1934 and operates as an independent U.S. government agency overseen by Congress." The FCC "is committed to being a responsive, efficient and effective agency capable of facing the technological and economic opportunities of the new millennium. In its work, the agency seeks to capitalize on its competencies in: Promoting competition, innovation, and investment in broadband services and facilities; supporting the nation's economy by ensuring an appropriate competitive framework for the unfolding of the communications revolution; encouraging the highest and best use of spectrum domestically and internationally; revising media regulations so that new technologies flourish alongside diversity and localism; [and] providing leadership in strengthening the defense of the nation's communications infrastructure." The FCC's website provides links to a vast array of resources for businesses and software developers, as well as consumers.

Media Matters for America
PO Box 52155, Washington, DC   20091
(202) 756-4100
website: www.mediamatters.org

Media Matters for America is a web-based nonprofit research organization that works to monitor and correct conservative misinformation and propaganda in print, television, radio, or the Internet media. It accomplishes this through opinion pieces, research, and in-depth studies of conservative programming and current issues of interest. On the Media Matters website, it features a blog to address breaking issues, video clips of instances of conservative misinformation, and its own programming to analyze pertinent stories. It also publishes a number of newsletters and media alerts that offer readers the latest news and updates on relevant stories.

Media Research Center (MRC)
325 S. Patrick St., Alexandria, VA   22314
(703) 683-9733 • fax: (703) 683-9736
website: www.mrc.org

The Media Research Center is a conservative watchdog group that monitors media, particularly television, for a liberal bias. Its aim is to expose and eliminate liberal leanings in television news programming. MRC publishes the opinion columns and studies of L. Brent Bozell III, as well as scientific research to back its claims of a pervasive liberal bias in mainstream media. On the MRC website is featured a blog to address breaking issues, video clips of television shows, and its own programming to analyze pertinent stories. It also publishes a number of newsletters that offer readers in-depth studies and research on media bias.

National Coalition Against Censorship (NCAC)
275 Seventh Ave., Ste. 1504, New York, NY   10001
(212) 807-6222 • fax: (212) 807-6245
e-mail: ncac@ncac.org
website: www.ncac.org

The National Coalition against Censorship is a network of fifty-two participating organizations that work together to support freedom of expression and to fight against censorship. NCAC accomplishes this through disseminating educational resources, offering support to individuals and organizations affected by censorship, documenting incidents of censorship, and lobbying the media and public about the dangers of censorship. It also provides research and studies on censorship issues and publishes a quarterly newsletter, *NCAC Censorship News*, that discusses current school censorship controversies, policies, and obscenity laws.

Parents Television Council (PTC)
707 Wilshire Blvd. #2075, Los Angeles, CA   90017
(800) 882-6868 • fax: (213) 403-1301
e-mail: editor@parentstv.org
website: www.parentstv.org

The Parents Television Council is an organization that aims to educate parents on TV content so they can make informed television-viewing decisions. PTC monitors television programs for excessive violence, sexual content, and indecent language and rates each program for easy reference. It publishes the *Family Guide to Primetime Television* and *PTC Picks* for concerned parents and viewers in search of family-friendly television. It also publishes in-depth studies on specific issues, such as the prevalence of violence on TV, representations of marriage on specific programs, and violence against women in many TV storylines. Weekly columns provide commentary on current controversies, and the monthly *PTC Insider* newsletter has "detailed accounts of ongoing campaigns, exclusive celebrity interviews, 'insider' reports on PTC events and press conferences, and previews of yet-to-be-released studies and Special Reports."

PolitiFact
490 First Ave. South, St. Petersburg, FL   33701
(727) 893-8111
website: www.politifact.com

A project of the *Tampa Bay Times*, PolitiFact has become a highly regarded fact-checking organization that analyzes statements by members of Congress, the White House, lobbyists, and interest groups. The reporters and editors that work on PolitiFact assesses the accuracy of this information, rating it on the Truth-o-Meter for its level of veracity. During the 2012 presidential election, for example, PolitiFact was very active in analyzing statements made on the campaign trail and during debates. The PolitiFact website offers access to weekly e-mail that offers updates and articles on recent analyses.

Society of Professional Journalists (SPJ)
3909 N. Meridian St., Indianapolis, IN   46208
(317) 927-8000 • fax: (317) 920-4789
website: www.spj.org

The Society of Professional Journalists is an organization dedicated to protecting a free and independent US press. SPJ also promotes high journalistic standards and ethical behavior; fosters excellence in journalism; encourages diversity and supports marginalized voices in media; and offers internships, training programs, and fellowships to develop a new generation of top journalists. SPJ provides a wealth of resources for journalists, including a job bank and a legal defense fund. The SPJ website features blogs, breaking news, and access to useful articles and other information for journalists.

Bibliography of Books

Glenn Beck *Cowards: What Politicians, Radicals, and the Media Refuse to Say*. New York: Threshold Editions, 2012.

Arthur Asa Berger *Media and Society: A Critical Perspective*. 3rd ed. Lanham, MD: Rowman & Littlefield, 2012.

David Folkenflik *Page One: Inside the* New York Times *and the Future of Journalism*. New York: PublicAffairs, 2011.

David Freddoso *Spin Masters: How the Media Ignored the Real News and Helped Reelect Barack Obama*. New York: Regnery, 2013.

Jason Gainous and Kevin M. Wagner *Rebooting American Politics: The Internet Revolution*. Lanham, MD: Rowman & Littlefield, 2011.

Tim Groseclose *Left Turn: How Liberal Media Bias Distorts the American Mind*. New York: St. Martin's, 2011.

Steven Hallock *The Press March to War: Newspapers Set the Stage for Military Intervention in Post–World War II America*. New York: Peter Lang, 2012.

Jennifer Holt *Empires of Entertainment: Media Industries and the Politics of Deregulation, 1980–1996*. New Brunswick, NJ: Rutgers University Press, 2011.

Henry Jenkins, Sam Ford, and Joshua Green — *Spreadable Media: Creating Value and Meaning in a Networked Culture.* New York: New York University Press, 2012.

Steven Johnson — *Future Perfect: The Case for Progress in a Networked Age.* New York: Riverhead Books, 2012.

Jonathan M. Ladd — *Why Americans Hate the Media and How It Matters.* Princeton, NJ: Princeton University Press, 2012.

Fred V. Lucas — *The Right Frequency: The Story of the Talk Radio Giants Who Shook Up the Political and Media Establishment.* Palisades, NY: History Publishing, 2012.

Robert W. McChesney — *The Political Economy of Media: Enduring Issues, Emerging Dilemmas.* New York: Monthly Review Press, 2008.

Sheila C. Murphy — *How Television Invented New Media.* New Brunswick, NJ: Rutgers University Press, 2011.

Rory O'Connor — *Friends, Followers, and the Future: How Social Media Are Changing Politics, Threatening Big Brands, and Killing Traditional Media.* San Francisco: City Lights Books, 2012.

Paul M. Poindexter — *Millennials, News, and Social Media: Is News Engagement a Thing of the Past?* New York: Peter Lang, 2012.

Frank Rose — *The Art of Immersion: How the Digital Generation Is Remaking Hollywood, Madison Avenue, and the Way We Tell Stories*. New York: Norton, 2011.

Jonathan Rosenbaum — *Goodbye Cinema, Hello Cinephilia: Film Culture in Transition*. Chicago: University of Chicago Press, 2010.

Pelle Snickars and Patrick Vonderau, eds. — *Moving Data: The iPhone and the Future of Media*. New York: Columbia University Press, 2012.

Teresa Tomeo — *Noise: How Our Media-Saturated Culture Dominates Lives and Dismantles Families*. West Chester, PA: Ascension, 2012.

Chuck Tyron — *On-Demand Culture: Digital Delivery and the Future of Movies*. New Brunswick, NJ: Rutgers University Press, 2013.

Rick Wilber, ed. — *Future Media*. San Francisco: Tachyon, 2011.

Index

G

H